D1301856

At Issue

| Can Diets Be Harmful?

Other Books in the At Issue Series:

At Issue

Can Diets Be Harmful?

Christine Watkins, Book Editor

GREENHAVEN PRESS
A part of Gale, Cengage Learning

Detroit • New York • San Francisco • New Haven, Conn • Waterville, Maine • London

Elizabeth Des Chenes, *Managing Editor*

© 2012 Greenhaven Press, a part of Gale, Cengage Learning.

Gale and Greenhaven Press are registered trademarks used herein under license.

For more information, contact:
Greenhaven Press
27500 Drake Rd.
Farmington Hills, MI 48331-3535
Or you can visit our Internet site at gale.cengage.com

For product information and technology assistance, contact us at

Gale Customer Support, 1-800-877-4253
For permission to use material from this text or product, submit all requests online at
www.cengage.com/permissions

Further permissions questions can be e-mailed to permissionrequest@cengage.com

Articles in Greenhaven Press anthologies are often edited for length to meet page requirements. In addition, original titles of these works are changed to clearly present the main thesis and to explicitly indicate the author's opinion. Every effort is made to ensure that Greenhaven Press accurately reflects the original intent of the authors. Every effort has been made to trace the owners of copyrighted material.

Cover image © Images.com/Corbis

LIBRARY OF CONGRESS CATALOGING-IN-PUBLICATION DATA

Can diets be harmful? / Christine Watkins, book editor.
   p. cm. -- (At issue)
   Includes bibliographical references and index.
   ISBN 978-0-7377-5556-5 (hardback) -- ISBN 978-0-7377-5557-2 (paperback)
   1. Reducing diets--Health aspects. 2. Diet in disease. I. Watkins, Christine.
   RM222.2.C27539 2011
   613.2'5--dc23
                                                                2011020813

Printed in the United States of America
1 2 3 4 5 6 7 15 14 13 12 11

Contents

Introduction

The diet and weight-loss industry has boomed in the past few decades with one out of three women and one out of four men on a diet at any given time. Americans spend billions of dollars on diet programs, diet books, and social dieting groups. In fact, it is estimated that the diet industry brings in between 40 to 100 billion dollars a year selling temporary weight loss products and programs. Yes, *temporary* weight loss, because statistics have shown that 95 percent of people who diet regain the weight they lose as a result of dieting within two years. One has to wonder: What is causing this preoccupation with dieting? And if so many Americans are on diets, why are 31 percent of adults obese and 15 percent of children and teenagers overweight?

To answer the first question, many experts look at the media. Television, magazines, newspapers, and movies tend to portray overweight characters as lazy or as people with few friends, while slender women and lean, muscular men are portrayed as sexy, popular, and successful. The advertising industry clearly promotes the idea that "thin is in," prompting many women, men, girls, and boys to correlate appearance with self-worth. As a result, an overriding preoccupation with body image leads some individuals into the realm of dieting, an exercise that often includes quick weight-loss programs that may produce more health problems than weight loss. Many "miracle" diets allow only one type of food, which deprive the body of important vitamins and minerals. Rapid weight loss can also result in dehydration and a loss of muscle density. Additionally, "one of the biggest dangers of dieting is that it is the swiftest route to disordered behavior and eating disorders," according to clinical psychologist Cari Corbet-Owen. As Dianne Neumark-Sztainer reports in her 2005 book "*I'm, Like, SO Fat!*", over one-half of teenage girls and nearly one-third of teenage boys use unhealthy weight control behaviors such as skipping meals, fasting, vomiting, and taking laxatives. And the website of the National Association of Anorexia Nervosa and Associated Disorders (ANAD) documents that 25 percent of college-aged women engage in bingeing and purging as a weight-management technique, and 35 percent of "normal dieters" progress to pathological dieting.

Turning to the second question, if so many Americans are on diets, why are they still gaining weight? Obesity has become a public health threat in America today and, according to the World Health Organization, is a crisis of "epidemic proportions." One explanation is that for many people, eating goes far beyond just an act in response to hunger and providing the body with necessary and proper nutrition. For some, the act of eating has an emotional or psychological component. The United States Department of Agriculture claims that the key to long-term weight loss is to focus on the psychological issues involved with eating habits. The licensed clinical psychologists and social workers at Cognitive Therapy Associates (CTA) agree. They report on their website, "Aside from what you eat, one must deal with where you eat, how you eat, when you eat, and why you eat. . . . This is the crux of the problem, and as long as one avoids the motivating issues, the behavior continues." Another explanation for why diets do not always succeed in keeping weight off is that dieting often involves restricting food intake to levels that leave a person feeling constantly hungry or deprived so that binge eating is almost irresistible. And binge eating can lead to yo-yo dieting, which is far worse for the body than carrying a little extra weight. Typically, the yo-yo dieter gains more weight than they lose, and more fat cells are accumulated in the process. From a health standpoint, experts believe that such extreme fluctuations in body weight may also increase the risk for coronary heart disease.

So, if diets are doomed to fail and can even be harmful, what can people do to lose weight and keep it off? "The challenge is to get the public to recognize that this is a health problem," says William Dietz, the director of the division of nutrition and physical activity in the National Center for Chronic Disease Prevention and Health Promotion at the Centers for Disease Control and Prevention. "I think that the American public still views obesity as a cosmetic problem." In other words, the emphasis must shift away from attaining an unrealistic "ideal" body image to becoming healthy, learning about nutrition, and making behavioral changes. David A. Kessler sums it up succinctly in his book *The End of Overeating: Taking Control of the Insatiable American Appetite*:

> "We now must face the reality that until we fundamentally alter our eating behavior, we will continue to squander billions of dollars on ineffective weight-loss schemes. The sooner we create and implement a framework that promotes prevention and treatment strategies that work, the sooner we will regain control over our minds and bodies. And then things can begin to change."

The authors in *At Issue: Can Diets Be Harmful?* discuss this and other issues concerning various diets and whether they are beneficial or detrimental to a person's physical, mental, and emotional health.

1

Dieting Can Cause Health Problems

Gretchen Voss

Gretchen Voss is an award-winning journalist and author.

Staying on a calorie-restricted diet to lose weight is difficult for many people; in fact, studies have shown that two-thirds of diet-ers regain more weight after discontinuing a diet than they ini-tially lost. This losing and gaining cycle—called "yo-yo dieting" or "weight cycling"—is detrimental to physical and emotional health. Metabolism and basic physiology, skin elasticity, arteries, the skeletal system, liver, heart, and the immune system can all be adversely affected from yo-yo dieting. Experts believe that successful and healthy weight loss can best be achieved through mental conditioning and behavioral change instead of following restrictive low-calorie diets.

All you have to do is wheel your grocery cart into a check-out line to see the cautionary tales screaming at you from the tabloids:

Kirstie Alley regained the 70-plus pounds she lost on Jenny Craig. Maureen "Marcia Brady" McCormick got even heavier after she was on "Celebrity Fit Club." Oprah—well, we all know about her struggles. Janet Jackson, Kelly Clarkson . . . the list goes on and on.

It makes you wonder: If these rich, powerful women, with their personal trainers and private chefs, can't win the weight war, what chance do I have?

It doesn't help that the statistics are grim: By some estimates, more than 80 percent of people who have lost weight regain all of it, or more, after two years. Researchers at the University of California at Los Angeles analyzed 31 long-term diet studies and found that about two-thirds of dieters regained more weight within four or five years than they initially lost.

Women who want to lose weight know these painful numbers all too well. "I've been on a roller coaster for the past two years," says Leigh Moyer, 31, of Philadelphia. In 2003, she lost 25 of her 155 pounds by diligently counting calories and logging daily sweat sessions at the gym. Four years later, busy with graduate school and her job at a software company, Leigh blew off her workouts and stopped monitoring her portions . . . and shot up to 175. "It was so sad, so frustrating," she says. "I let myself down."

Along with the emotional toll is a physical one: Not only is the extra weight a health risk, but recent studies have linked the gain-lose-gain cycle to such potentially life-threatening conditions as high blood pressure, high cholesterol, diabetes, depression, heart disease, and cancer.

[T]wo-thirds of dieters regained more weight . . . than they initially lost.

Yo-Yo Dieting

While small fluctuations on the scale are normal, the unhealthy behavior that experts refer to as "weight cycling" is not. Cycling is defined as a significant increase or decrease of body weight (generally 10 pounds or more) that occurs multiple times.

Experts believe a yo-yo pattern is often the result of a diet that's too restrictive, and a study reported in the journal *Obesity* backs that up: It found that people who followed a very low-calorie diet regained significantly more weight than those on a more forgiving plan. Desperate for quick results in a culture of instant gratification, "women try to lose weight on diets with too few calories," says Judith Beck, Ph.D., director of the Beck Institute of Cognitive Therapy and author of *The Beck Diet Solution.* "If you lose weight on 1,200 calories a day, the minute you go up to 1,300 is the minute you start gaining weight."

It happened to Tracy Srail. The 24-year-old from Atlanta has watched the scale bounce between 130 and 160 pounds for the past four years. "At one point, I was eating only one or two meals a day and chugging Rockstar energy drinks because I heard that caffeine increases your metabolism. I lost 15 pounds, but it didn't stick," she says. "I weigh about 155 now."

Even on a sensible diet, your body sheds pounds reluctantly. "One reason it's difficult to keep weight off is because there is a metabolic overcompensation for weight loss," says Gary Foster, Ph.D., director of the Center of Obesity Research and Education at Temple University in Philadelphia. "If you decrease your body mass by 10 percent, you would expect your metabolic rate to decrease by 10 percent, but it actually slows down more than that, by about 11 to 15 percent."

Why does your own metabolism thwart you? Simple, says Kelly Brownell, M.D., director of the Rudd Center for Food Policy and Obesity at Yale University: "The body may perceive dieting as a threat to its survival. It might not know the difference between Atkins and famine."

What's more, says Brownell, who coined the term "yo-yo dieting" in the 1980s, weight cycling can actually change your physiology. So the more diets you've been on, the harder it becomes to lose the weight. A hunger hormone called ghrelin increases, and a fullness hormone called leptin decreases, so you feel hungrier and less satiated.

It's bad enough that your body fights you when you try to lose weight. Now there's compelling research to show that some people may be hardwired to yo-yo.

"Conditioned Hypereaters"

David Kessler, M.D., former U.S. Food and Drug Administration commissioner and author of *The End of Overeating*, and his team of researchers at the University of California at San Francisco and Yale University looked into the biology of weight cycling. They found that the reward circuits in the brains of people Kessler calls "conditioned hypereaters" were excessively activated simply by the smell of food and stayed that way until those people finished eating whatever was on the plate in front of them.

[T]he more diets you've been on, the harder it becomes to lose the weight.

In other words, when you have overactive neural circuitry, resisting temptation is not a question of willpower alone. "This is a biological cause of conditioned hypereating. It's the first time we can say 'It's not your fault,'" Kessler says. He estimates that 50 percent of obese people and 30 percent of overweight people are conditioned hypereaters.

Evidence shows, however, that this reaction is partially learned, and that through conditioning, you can rewire your brain. After all, the yen to yo-yo is not just physical; emotional triggers play a huge role too. A study at Brown University found that dieters who ate in response to emotions such as stress or loneliness—as opposed to external events, like overdoing it at happy hour—were more likely to regain weight.

When Darcie Schmidt of Sioux Falls, South Dakota, was in her late twenties, she lost 75 pounds and then regained 120 over two years, largely because of emotional eating, she says. In her early thirties, she stuck to a strict diet-and-exercise regimen and shed 132 pounds. "I did not eat a single chip for 18 months," she says. But the stress of a divorce, a move, and a return to school knocked her off track, and she traded her three-mile, five-day-a-week runs for bags of those verboten chips—and regained 40 pounds.

Beck sees women like Schmidt all the time, who do well for a while, only to fall off the wagon. The problem, she believes, is that they never learned the skills needed for long-term behavior change. "They haven't been taught how to motivate themselves every day," Beck says, "or how to respond to negative thoughts and recognize a mistake as a one-time thing."

A study of 200 overweight and obese people, published in the *Journal of Psychosomatic Research*, supports the importance of a behavior-change approach. Along with other weight-loss techniques, one group received an additional hour of therapy, in which they learned to change their behavior; the other group did an extra hour of low-intensity exercise. After a year, those in the therapy group had maintained their weight loss, while the other group's members hadn't.

[W]omen who weight cycle five times or more during their lifetimes may be damaging their hearts. . . .

Risky Bigness

While watching the numbers on the scale fluctuate wildly is a blues inducer and clothes-budget buster, there are far more compelling reasons to hold steady. For one, your metabolism might be affected—and not in the way you probably hoped.

"If you go on a very strict diet and gain the weight back quickly, you might lose a lot of muscle and regain a lot of fat," says Keith Ayoob, M.D., R.D., an associate professor at the Albert Einstein College of Medicine. "Then your metabolism operates on a slower idle, which means it's going to be harder to lose weight as time goes on."

The more times you yo-yo, the theory goes, the more fat your body gains in each rebound. Because muscle burns 10 times more calories than fat does, your metabolism eventually will slow to a crawl.

"Losing and gaining regularly takes a huge toll on your body," Ayoob says. Beyond aesthetics, such as a loss of skin elasticity, regaining weight burdens your arteries and skeletal system, and may stress the liver, which can become covered in fat.

Yo-yoing also does a number on your ticker: A study in *Clinical Cardiology* found that women who weight cycle five times or more during their lifetimes may be damaging their hearts in the process.

But perhaps most startling is the dangerous and lasting effect weight cycling has on the immune system. According to the first study of the long-term impacts of yo-yo dieting, women who repeatedly lost and gained weight had lower immune function, particularly lower counts of natural killer cells. "These cells are important for fending off infections and are also vital in fighting the early stages of cancer," says Cornelia Ulrich, M.D., of the Fred Hutchinson Cancer Research Center in Seattle. Low killer-cell activity is associated with higher rates of cancer. In her study of more than a hundred overweight but otherwise healthy women, those who had yo-yoed most frequently—five times or more—decreased their natural killer-cell activity by a third. . . .

2

Calorie Restriction Improves and Extends Life

Paul McGlothin and Meredith Averill

Paul McGlothin and Meredith Averill, leaders of the Calorie Restriction Society, have practiced calorie restriction for over fifteen years. They have been featured on the television news programs Good Morning America, *the* Today Show, 20/20, *and* CBS News, *as well as in* New York Magazine, Fortune, *and other publications.*

Scientific research has documented that calorie restriction (CR) slows the aging process and provides a broad range of health benefits. Feeding the body fewer calories forces it to adapt and become more efficient at producing energy and utilizing nutrients. At the same time, fewer calories mean less excess waste that would normally add stress and disease to the body. As a result of the increased efficiency, cell reproduction is enhanced, dysfunctional and unhealthy cells are eliminated, and youthful hormones are preserved.

The search for the fabled Fountain of Youth symbolizes the desire to remain young that has been a sought-after goal throughout history. It has been thought to be truly unattainable. Little did we know that the mythical waters of youth have resided within us all along. The human body is an amazing, resilient machine, shown to survive and thrive no matter what the external forces may be. Our evolutionary road has been a long, sometimes harsh one and yet we've adapted and flourished. How?

Researchers postulate that when our ancestors struggled through extended periods without food, the body's remarkable survival instinct would kick in and somehow slow down their aging. This allowed our species to live through difficult times—responding to hardships and challenges by becoming stronger and more resilient. The common thread appears to have been food, or rather, lack of food. The fact that consuming fewer calories somehow slowed the aging process has inspired scientific research for many decades. Most recently, science has begun to shine a light on what is happening on the genetic level.

Since the 1930s, when Dr. Clive McKay's breakthrough studies showed that calorie restriction [CR] greatly extended the lives of mice, scientists have been trying to discover how calorie restriction works. Thousands of studies have documented the broad range of health and longevity benefits of calorie restriction, but most theories on how it slows aging focus on only one of CR's many effects.

For example, identified effects of calorie restriction include:

- More effective disposal and renewal of cells

- Preservation of irreplaceable cells

- Reduced rate of growth

- More efficient energy production, including increased formation of mitochondria, the cells' energy generators

- Enhanced DNA [deoxyribonucleic acid] stability

- Reduction of age-related decline of the immune system

Each is a positive health benefit and may contribute to longevity. However, a theory has emerged—hormesis—that explains these positive effects (and many others) of calorie restriction as the body's natural response to the low-level biological stress produced by reduced food intake.

> [W]hen you limit your intake of calories intelligently, you challenge your body with a beneficial stress. . . .

Beneficial Stress

Just think about weight lifters who want to build their biceps. They determine a workout schedule with weights heavy enough to stress their arm muscles but not so heavy that they produce injury. The bodybuilders challenge the biceps with a form of hormesis, purposely pushing the muscle just beyond the standard, day-to-day activity to strengthen it. So we manage our amount of hormesis.

Now compare overeating to limiting calories intelligently: When you eat more calories or food energy than you need, your body often must cope with the added fuel by secreting insulin to process the high glucose levels circulating in your bloodstream. Some of the excess is stored for future use. But much of it is simply not needed, so it can end up being stored as fat tissue or deposited as plaque in your arteries. With so much food intake, your body does not need to use it efficiently, so your cells may run amok. Their job of reproducing themselves can be disrupted, sometimes resulting in unregulated cell reproduction that, in turn, can become cancerous cell growth. Your pancreas—the digestive organ that produces insulin—works overtime and becomes less able to do its job, and your heart beats more stressfully just to circulate blood to the extra tissue.

In contrast, when you limit your intake of calories intelligently, you challenge you body with a beneficial stress, or *hormesis*. With fewer calories available for energy production, your body shifts away from storing fat to actually using fat as well as protein for energy. Soon you cells produce energy more efficiently and your stamina increases. Meanwhile, cell reproduction slows—giving the body time to protect against mutations and preserving cells that may be irreplaceable. As your body continues to adapt, you get stronger—becoming more resistant to disease and the deterioration caused by aging. . . .

Many aging regulators have been discovered—some speeding and some slowing the aging process. What is important to know about these aging regulators is that they share a common "theme"—nutrient sensitivity. They are activated by more or less food availability, and some of those that accelerate aging are activated, independent of total calories, by high levels of glucose or protein.

Biological Effects of Glucose

CR consistently produces biological effects that are linked in laboratory animals to longer life. Understanding the "themes" of these biological effects helps enormously in practically applying the knowledge to lifestyle choices and in gaining maximum benefit from CR. Some major CR effects were identified in early research. More have been discovered in recent years. And we now know that we can affect many of them by our individual choices.

Here are the major CR effects that are important to understand . . .

- CR lowers circulating glucose and insulin levels

- CR reduces body fat

- CR lowers levels of growth stimulators

- CR prevents cell loss

- CR decreases inflammation

- CR creates a more youthful physiology

Blood glucose, also commonly known as "blood sugar," circulates through the body by way of the blood and lymphatic systems, and is the major source of energy in the body. When circulating glucose levels rise, the hormone insulin is released within minutes and helps glucose enter the cells. Insulin converts glucose into glycogen, the major carbohydrate reserve of animals. Additional insulin actions include stimulation of protein synthesis, formation of fat tissue, and increased cell growth. Sound like a 100 percent true-blue friend?

Calorie restriction causes glucose and insulin levels to fall.

The more glucose you have circulating through your blood, the more insulin will be released to help regulate the blood sugar. High circulating levels of glucose and insulin are associated with accelerated aging and disease. In fact, high levels of both glucose and insulin have been independently documented as predictors of death rates.

Witness the staggering incidence of diabetes, a disease in which the body either fails to produce sufficient amounts of insulin, or is unable to use it properly to process the body's glucose. With more than 7 percent of the population of the United States, or 20.8 million children and adults living with diabetes, according to the American Diabetes Association, almost everyone is familiar with the frequent complications of Type II diabetes: Glucose levels that spiral out of control produce effects such as an increased incidence of cardiovascular disease, macular degeneration, nerve damage, and kidney disease.

Calorie restriction causes glucose and insulin levels to fall. The normal range for glucose levels—measured as fasting glucose, which is simply the level of glucose in your blood after you have not eaten for eight hours—is lower than 100 milligrams/deciliter (mg/dl). Calorie restriction will likely reduce this measurement. When glucose levels fall into the 80s or below, insulin production shuts down so glucose does not fall further.

Like a thermostat that turns on the furnace when the temperature falls, the SIRT1 longevity gene becomes active when glucose reaches this low level. This facilitates the burning of fats and proteins for fuel while reducing the risks of heart disease, inflammation, diabetes, and other age-related illnesses. . . .

Some may think that CR's lower blood sugar levels mean that you would have less energy. Just the opposite happens: You will feel *more* energetic. As cells adapt to the low food supply, they create more energy producers, or mitochondria, and you will see the result: huge increases in stamina. Life becomes happier and more productive as your new high-energy state makes everything easier.

Cells will also use energy more efficiently, so the body benefits more from the smaller amount of food that's available. . . .

Cell Reproduction

As one ages, the body's ability to produce new cells decreases. As cells die, the inability of the body to replace them is thought by some to be at the root of aging—and of several age-related diseases. For example, researchers at Duke University found that older mice were unable to produce new cells that repair arteries, thereby causing atherosclerosis, the artery-blocking disease. Proving the point—when the old mice were injected with cells from younger animals, their repair processes immediately functioned normally.

Much research has been done on mice over the decades, showing that calorie restriction preserves their ability, as they age, to reproduce cells at youthful levels.

Does CR preserve the ability to reproduce cells at youthful levels in humans? Thanks to a collaboration between the Calorie Restriction Society and scientists at Washington University, led by Assistant Professor Luigi Fontana, M.D., Ph.D., we may soon know more about CR effects in humans. Dramatic results of CR's ability to prevent atherosclerosis in humans have been shown in a breakthrough study .... Plaque accumulation was found to be 40 percent lower in the arteries of the CR group versus the controls.

CR is instrumental in . . . increasing the number of newly generated brain cells. . . .

Measuring the thickness of the carotid artery in the neck, an indicator of plaque buildup, can help predict coronary artery disease. The thicker the inner and middle layers, measured in millimeters, the thicker the artery walls and the greater the chance of atherosclerosis.

Like the mythological Greek god Zeus, granting the mortal Tithonus eternal life but not eternal youth, it would be a cruel joke to slow the body's aging process without including the mind.

Some of the most exciting research today shows calorie restriction rejuvenating nerve cells. This would increase the brain's capability for repair and cognition. Dr. Mark Mattson, renowned scientist and fellow CR practitioner, conducted research into CR's ability to rejuvenate new cells. His data suggest that CR is instrumental in 1) increasing the number of newly generated brain cells and 2) along with physical and mental activity possibly reducing the incidence and severity of human neuro-degenerative disorders.

Applying Dr. Mattson's research by practicing CR has produced measurable cognitive benefits—better long- and short-term memories, and sharper awareness in everything we do. By incorporating cognitive testing into your CR lifestyle through brain games, you will realize remarkable cognitive improvement. Learning to speak another language or to play a musical instrument has a good reputation for brain training. Measuring the results is easier, though, with mental proficiency exercises.

Disposing of malfunctioning cells through programmed cell death—which increases with age—is an important physiological process that helps maintain healthy cells.

Imagine a snake shedding its skin. The old, dead cells are sloughed off, and what emerges is a sleek, healthy, glistening creature: nature's own facelift. In tissues that are rapidly dividing—like skin, for example—CR increases the rate of this cell turnover, perhaps improving the health of the skin by hastening the death of dysfunctional cells.

Normally the body senses which cells are unhealthy and kills them before they have a chance to create dangerous mutations. As we get older, elimination of bad cells becomes less efficient. CR prevents this age-related decline in efficiency by increasing the rate of cell disposal of precancerous cells, which may be one of the ways CR protects against cancer, according to research by Dr. Stephen Spindler, one of the world's leading calorie restriction scientists.

Other leaders in this field, Drs. Haim Cohen and David Sinclair, proposed in a 2004 study that CR maintains physiological function by activating our hero, SIRT1, which protects necessary cells from dying off, thereby promoting the long-term survival of important, irreplaceable cells. . . .

3

Claims That Calorie Restricted Diets Extend Life Are Exaggerated

Tom Venuto

Tom Venuto is a fat loss expert, bodybuilder, nutrition researcher, and author of the diet e-book Burn the Fat, Feed the Muscle *and the book* The Body Fat Solution.

Because studies have shown that calorie-restricted diets have increased the lifespan of certain animals, speculation has grown that calorie restriction (CR) can increase the lifespan of human beings as well. No direct experimental evidence exists, however, that shows whether CR can extend human life, and if so, by how much. In fact, many experts believe any increase would be so slight that it would not be worth the hunger and discomfort involved. A proven and more practical approach to health and longevity is to increase physical activity and eat only highly nutritious, low-calorie food.

On a[n] . . . episode of the *Oprah* show, one of the guests was a 51-year-old man with the heart of a 20-year-old. He's been following a "calorie restriction" [CR] plan and they said he might be one of the first people to reach 120 years old by following this plan. There have been stories both in the lay press and scientific press about CR for years and it has been a frequent talk show topic on many other TV shows. However, before you cut your calories in half in hopes of adding another decade onto your life, you'd better get the other half of the story they didn't talk about on *Oprah.*

I've seen a lot of strange things in the health field, and although CR is the subject of serious and legitimate scientific study, I consider CR to be one of those strange things. Of course, that's because I choose a different lifestyle—the muscle-friendly *Burn The Fat, Feed The Muscle* [diet e-book] lifestyle—but there's more than one reason why I'm not a CR advocate.

Hunger while dieting is almost always a challenge. There's some hunger even with conservative calorie deficits of 15–20% under maintenance. Prolonged hunger is one of the biggest reasons people fall off the weight loss diet wagon because it's unpleasant and difficult to resist. This is why pharmaceutical and supplement companies spend millions of dollars on researching, developing and marketing appetite suppressants. Yet CR advocates put themselves through 30–50% calorie restriction on a daily basis as a way of life in the hopes of extending life span or health.

Speculative Research

Practitioners of CR follow a low-calorie lifestyle, but technically, they are not in a chronic 30% calorie deficit. That would be impossible. What happens is their metabolisms get very slow (that's part of the idea behind CR; if you slow down your metabolism, you allegedly slow down aging). So a 6-foot-tall man who would normally require nearly 3,000 calories to maintain his weight might eventually reach an energy balance at only 1800 or 1900 calories. This is not just due to a "starvation mode" phenomenon; that's only part of it. It's primarily because he loses weight until he is very thin and his smaller body doesn't need many calories any more.

The biological mechanisms of lifespan extension through CR are not fully understood, but researchers say it may involve alterations in energy metabolism (as mentioned above), reduced oxidative damage, improvements in insulin sensitivity, reduction of glycation, modulation of protein metabolism, downregulation of pro-inflammatory genes and functional changes in both neuroendocrine and autonomic nervous systems.

Mouse studies on CR go back as far as 1935 and monkey studies began in the late 1980's. So far the results are clear on one thing: caloric restriction does increase lifespan in rodents and other lower species (yeast, worms and flies). Studies suggest the life of the laboratory rat is 25% longer with CR (even longer with aggressive CR). Primate studies are still underway and humans have been experimenting with CR for some time. In primates and humans, biomarkers of aging show signs of slower aging with CR. This makes many proponents talk about this CR as if it were a sure thing, already proven through double-blind randomized clinical human trials.

The truth is, there is NO direct experimental evidence that you will live longer from practicing CR. Due to the length of human lifespans, we will not have the necessary data for at least another generation and perhaps multiple generations. Even then, it will still be highly speculative whether CR will extend human life at all and if so how much. We can only estimate. I've seen guesses in the scientific literature ranging from 3 to 13 years, if CR is practiced for an entire adult lifetime.

Jay Phelan, a biologist at UCLA [University of California, Los Angeles] is skeptical. He says the potential life extension is on the lower end of that range and the increase is so small that it's not worth the semi-starvation:

"There is no current evidence that lifelong caloric restriction leads to increased lifespan in primates. It's certainly tantalizing that things like blood pressure or heart rate look as though they are a lot healthier and I believe they are. Whether or not this translates to a significantly increased lifespan, I don't know. I predict that it doesn't."

"I don't quibble qualitatively with their results. Yes, it will increase lifespan, but it will not increase it by 50% or 60%, it won't increase it by 20% or 10%, it might increase it by 2%. So if you tell me that I have to do something horrible for every day of my life for a 2% benefit—for an extra year of life—I say no thanks."

Perpetual Hunger

When caloric restriction is practiced with optimal nutrition (CRON), it is not inherently unhealthy. Actually, it appears the reverse is true. First, the weight loss that comes with the low calories produces improvements in the health markers, as you would expect. Second, the meticulous choice of food from CRON practitioners, where they pick high nutrient foods and avoid empty calories means that they are making healthy food choices. Third, advocates say that the CR itself improves health. I wonder, however, how much does CR improve health independent of the weight loss and the optimal nutrition?

Maybe we ought to be focusing more on "health span" than lifespan.

By losing fat and maintaining an ideal body composition (the fat to muscle ratio) and eating high-nutrient density foods, I propose that even at a more normal caloric intake, you will get very significant health and longevity benefits. I also propose that gaining muscle in a natural way (no steroids) will increase your quality of life today and as you get older.

Aside from the fact that we are not lab rats, the truth is, none of us knows when our day will come. We could get plucked off this physical plane at any moment and have no control over how it happens. My belief is that we should make our lifestyle decisions based on quality of life, not just quantity of life. That includes our quality of life today as well as our anticipated quality of life when we are older. Maybe we ought to be focusing more on "health span" than life span.

One fact about CR that they often don't mention on these talk shows is that the benefits of CR decline if you start CR at a later age. This was discussed in a research paper from the *Journal of Nutrition* called, "Starving for life: what animal studies can and cannot tell us about the use of caloric restriction to prolong human lifespan." The author of the paper, John Speakman from the School of Biological Sciences at the University of Aberdeen in Scotland, said that the later in life you begin to practice CR, the less of an increase in lifespan you will achieve. Even if the CR proponents are right, if you started in your late 40's or mid 50's for example, the benefit would be minimal. If you started in your 60's the effect would be almost nonexistent. Essentially, you have to "starve for life" to get the benefits.

While some CR proponents claim that they aren't hungry and they cite studies suggesting that hunger decreases during starvation, Speakman and other researchers say that hunger remains a big problem during CR—especially in today's modern society where we are surrounded with convenience food and numerous eating cues—and that alone makes CR impractical:

> "*Neuroendocrine profiles support the idea that animals under CR are continuously hungry. The feasibility of restricting intake in humans for many decades is questionable.*"

Health Concerns

Let's suppose for a moment that CR is totally legit and the claims are true. Many of the proposed benefits of CR come at the expense of what many of us are trying to do here: gain and maintain lean body mass. One spokesman for CR is 6 feet tall and 130 pounds. Another poster boy for CR is 6-foot-tall and 115 lbs. Measurements of rodents under CR not only show large reductions in skeletal muscle but also bone mass.

I am not suggesting that these CR practitioners are anorexic, a concern that has been raised about CR when practiced aggressively. However, they are losing large amounts of fat-free tissue and that is plainly obvious for all to see when you look at their bony physiques. I am not imposing my body standards on others, but 115 to 130 lbs at 6 foot tall is underweight for a man by any standard. Furthermore, researchers say that at the body mass indices sustained by most voluntary CR practitioners, we would expect females to become amenorrheic [having no menstrual cycle]. "One thing that is completely incompatible with a CR lifestyle is reproduction" says Speakman.

With that kind of atrophy, I have to wonder what their quality of life will be like in old age. While many people struggle with body fat for most of their adult lives, I'm sure almost everyone knows an elderly person who wrestles with the opposite problem: they are seriously underweight and they struggle to eat enough and maintain lean body mass.

My grandmother, before she passed away, was under 80 lbs. We could not get her to eat. She was weak and very frail. I have reported many times about the research showing how most overweight people underestimate calorie intake and eat more than they think or admit. In elder care homes, the research has often showed the opposite—the patients overestimate how much they eat. They swear they are eating enough, but they aren't and they keep losing dangerous amounts of weight. With underweight, atrophied seniors, weakness means less functionality and lower quality of life and a fall can mean more than broken bones, it can be life threatening.

More Practical Options

While there is a commonality between CRON and the way I recommend eating (high nutrient density, low calorie density foods), in most regards, CR is the opposite of my approach. In my *Burn The Fat, Feed The Muscle program*, we go for a higher energy flux nutrition program, which means that because we are weight training and doing cardio and leading a very active lifestyle, we get to eat more. Because we are so active and well-trained, the eating more does not have a negative effect as it would on a sedentary person, who might get sick and fat from the additional calories. We active folks take those calories, burn them for energy, partition them into lean muscle tissue and we enjoy a faster metabolism and extremely high quality of life.

As a bodybuilder, CR is not compatible with my priorities, but hypothetically speaking, if I were to practice a lower calorie lifestyle, I wouldn't follow an aggressive CR approach. I'd probably do as the Okinawans do. They have a very simple philosophy: hari hachi bu: eat until you are only 80% full. While this does not mean there is a carefully measured 20% calorie deficit, it's consistent with what we practice in the *Burn The Fat, Feed The Muscle* lifestyle for a fat loss phase, and avoiding overeating is certainly a smart way to avoid obesity and health problems. Incidentally, the Okinawans eat about 40% less than Americans, and 11% less than they should, according to standard caloric intake guidelines, and they live 4 years longer than Americans.

CR for humans remains highly controversial and there are no guarantees that this will extend your life.

If someone is being "sold" on CR by an enthusiastic CR spokesperson, or simply curious after watching the latest TV talk show (where they are looking for controversial stories), it's important to know that there is more than one side to the story. If you carefully read the entire body of research on CR, you will see that the experts are split right down the middle in their opinions about whether CR will really work. CR for humans remains highly controversial and there are no guarantees that this will extend your life.

Researchers at the National Institutes of Health in Baltimore, MD put it this way:

"Because it is unlikely that an experimental study will ever be designed to address this question in humans, we respond that we think we will never know for sure. We suggest that debate of this question is clearly an academic exercise." . . .

I believe that by making healthy food choices but doing so at a higher level of calorie intake and expenditure, that we can fend off sarcopenia—the age related decline in muscle mass that debilitates many seniors—while enjoying a more muscular physique, greater strength, and a less restrictive lifestyle. Most gerontologists agree—by making simple lifestyle changes that include strength training and good nutrition, you can easily turn back the biological clock 10 years without going hungry.

4

Vegetarian Diets Help Prevent Disease

Winston J. Craig and Ann Reed Mangels

Winston J. Craig is professor of nutrition and director of the dietetics internship program at Andrews University in Berrien Springs, Michigan. Ann Reed Mangels, a registered dietitian, is the nutrition advisor for the Vegetarian Resource Group, a nonprofit organization based in Baltimore, Maryland.

Studies have found that vegetarians tend to have lower overall cancer rates, as well as a lower risk of heart disease, diabetes, and obesity than nonvegetarians. Such health advantages may be partly explained by the nutritional differences between plant foods and animal-based foods. For example, vegetarian diets are lower in saturated fat and cholesterol and have higher levels of dietary fiber, vitamins C and E, flavonoids, and phytochemicals. Furthermore, well-planned vegetarian diets are appropriate for all stages of life, including infancy, adolescence, pregnancy, and older adulthood.

Vegetarian diets are often associated with a number of health advantages, including lower blood cholesterol levels, lower risk of heart disease, lower blood pressure levels, and lower risk of hypertension and type 2 diabetes. Vegetarians tend to have a lower body mass index (BMI) and lower overall cancer rates. Vegetarian diets tend to be lower in saturated fat and cholesterol, and have higher levels of dietary fiber, magnesium and potassium, vitamins C and E, folate, carotenoids, flavonoids, and other phytochemicals. These nutritional differences may explain some of the health advantages of those following a varied, balanced vegetarian diet. However, vegans and some other vegetarians may have lower intakes of vitamin B-12, calcium, vitamin D, zinc, and long-chain n-3 fatty acids. . . .

Vegetarian Diets Throughout the Life Cycle

Well-planned vegan [excludes eggs, dairy, and all other animal products], lacto-vegetarian [allows dairy], and lacto-ovo-vegetarian [allows dairy and eggs] diets are appropriate for all stages of the life cycle, including pregnancy and lactation. Appropriately planned vegan, lacto-vegetarian, and lacto-ovo-vegetarian diets satisfy nutrient needs of infants, children, and adolescents and promote normal growth. . . . Lifelong vegetarians have adult height, weight, and BMIs that are similar to those who became vegetarian later in life, suggesting that well-planned vegetarian diets in infancy and childhood do not affect final adult height or weight. Vegetarian diets in childhood and adolescence can aid in the establishment of lifelong healthful eating patterns and can offer some important nutritional advantages. Vegetarian children and adolescents have lower intakes of cholesterol, saturated fat, and total fat and higher intakes of fruits, vegetables, and fiber than nonvegetarians. Vegetarian children have also been reported to be leaner and to have lower serum cholesterol levels.

The nutrient and energy needs of pregnant and lactating vegetarian women do not differ from those of nonvegetarian women with the exception of higher iron recommendations for vegetarians. Vegetarian diets can be planned to meet the nutrient needs of pregnant and lactating women. . . .

Vegetarian Diets Protect Against Hypertension

A cross-sectional study and a cohort study found that there was a lower rate of hypertension among vegetarians than non-vegetarians. Similar findings were reported in Seventh-Day Adventists (Adventists) in Barbados and in preliminary results from the Adventist Health Study-2 cohort. Vegans appear to have a lower rate of hypertension than do other vegetarians.

Several studies have reported lower blood pressure in vegetarians compared to nonvegetarians although other studies reported little difference in blood pressure between vegetarians and nonvegetarians. At least one of the studies reporting lower blood pressure in vegetarians found that BMI rather than diet accounted for much of the age-adjusted variation in blood pressure. Vegetarians tend to have a lower BMI than nonvegetarians; thus, vegetarian diets' influence on BMI may partially account for reported differences in blood pressure between vegetarians and nonvegetarians. Variations in dietary intake and lifestyle within groups of vegetarians may limit the strength of conclusions with regard to the relationship between vegetarian diets and blood pressure.

Vegetarians tend to have an overall cancer rate lower than that of the general population. . . .

Possible factors in vegetarian diets that could result in lower blood pressure include the collective effect of various beneficial compounds found in plant foods such as potassium, magnesium, antioxidants, dietary fat, and fiber. Results from the Dietary Approaches to Stop Hypertension study, in which subjects consumed a low-fat diet rich in fruits, vegetables, and dairy, suggest that substantial dietary levels of potassium, magnesium, and calcium play an important role in reducing blood pressure levels. Fruit and vegetable intake was responsible for about one-half of the blood pressure reduction of the

Dietary Approaches to Stop Hypertension diet. In addition, nine studies report that consumption of five to 10 servings of fruit and vegetables significantly lowers blood pressure.

Vegetarian Diets Protect Against Diabetes

Adventist vegetarians are reported to have lower rates of diabetes than Adventist nonvegetarians. In the Adventist Health Study, age-adjusted risk for developing diabetes was two-fold greater in nonvegetarians, compared with their vegetarian counterparts. Although obesity increases the risk of type 2 diabetes, meat and processed meat intake was found to be an important risk factor for diabetes even after adjustment for BMI. In the Women's Health Study, the authors also observed positive associations between intakes of red meat and processed meat and risk of diabetes after adjusting for BMI, total energy intake, and exercise. A significantly increased risk of diabetes was most pronounced for frequent consumption of processed meats such as bacon and hot dogs. Results remained significant even after further adjustment for dietary fiber, magnesium, fat, and glycemic load. In a large cohort study, the relative risk for type 2 diabetes in women for every one-serving increase in intake was 1.26 for red meat and 1.38 to 1.73 for processed meats.

In addition, higher intakes of vegetables, whole-grain foods, legumes, and nuts have all been associated with a substantially lower risk of insulin resistance and type 2 diabetes, and improved glycemic control in either normal or insulin-resistant individuals. Observational studies have found that diets rich in whole-grain foods are associated with improved insulin sensitivity. . . .

Vegetarian Diets Protect Against Cancer

Vegetarians tend to have an overall cancer rate lower than that of the general population, and this is not confined to smoking-related cancers. Data from the Adventist Health Study revealed that nonvegetarians had a substantially increased risk for both colorectal and prostate cancer compared with vegetarians, but there were no significant differences in risk of lung, breast, uterine, or stomach cancer between the groups after controlling for age, sex, and smoking. Obesity is a significant factor increasing the risk of cancer at a number of sites. Because the BMI [body mass index] of vegetarians tends to be lower than that of nonvegetarians, the lighter body weight of the vegetarians may be an important factor.

A vegetarian diet provides a variety of cancer-protective dietary factors. Epidemiologic studies have consistently shown that a regular consumption of fruit and vegetables is strongly associated with a reduced risk of some cancers. In contrast, among survivors of early stage breast cancer in the Women's Healthy Eating and Living trial, the adoption of a diet enhanced by additional daily fruit and vegetable servings did not reduce additional breast cancer events or mortality over a 7-year period.

Fruit and vegetables contain a complex mixture of phytochemicals, possessing potent antioxidant, antiproliferative, and cancer-protective activity. The phytochemicals can display additive and synergistic effects, and are best consumed in whole foods. These phytochemicals interfere with several cellular processes involved in the progression of cancer. . . .

According to the recent World Cancer Research Fund report, fruit and vegetables are protective against cancer of the lung, mouth, esophagus, and stomach, and to a lesser degree some other sites. The regular use of legumes also provides a measure of protection against stomach and prostate cancer. Fiber, vitamin C, carotenoids, flavonoids, and other phytochemicals in the diet are reported to exhibit protection against various cancers. Allium vegetables may protect against stomach cancer and garlic protects against colorectal cancer. Fruits rich in the red pigment lycopene are reported to protect against prostate cancer. Recently, cohort studies have suggested that a high intake of whole grains provided substantial protection against various cancers. Regular physical activity provides significant protection against most of the major cancers. . . .

Other Health Effects of Vegetarian Diets

In a cohort study, middle-aged vegetarians were found to be 50% less likely to have diverticulitis compared with nonvegetarians. Fiber was considered to be the most important protective factor, whereas meat intake may increase the risk of diverticulitis. In a cohort study of 800 women aged 40 to 69 years, nonvegetarians were more than twice as likely as vegetarians to suffer from gallstones, even after controlling for obesity, sex, and aging. Several studies from a research group in Finland suggest that fasting, followed by a vegan diet, may be useful in the treatment of rheumatoid arthritis. . . .

Appropriately planned vegetarian diets have been shown to be healthful, nutritionally adequate, and may be beneficial in the prevention and treatment of certain diseases. Vegetarian diets are appropriate for all stages of the life cycle. There are many reasons for the rising interest in vegetarian diets. The number of vegetarians in the United States is expected to increase during the next decade. Food and nutrition professionals can assist vegetarian clients by providing current, accurate information about vegetarian nutrition, foods, and resources.

5

Vegetarian Diets Can Be Problematic

Victoria Anisman-Reiner

Victoria Anisman-Reiner is a writer and teacher in holistic health and energy healing. She has written articles for a variety of websites and print publications.

A vegetarian diet can be beneficial for a person's health, but it can also be detrimental if not carefully planned and researched. Adequate amounts of essential amino acids—usually obtained from meat for nonvegetarians—are vital for mental and physical health. Likewise, vitamin B12, which is necessary for energy and robust mental function, cannot be absorbed from plant sources. Furthermore, some health professionals actually consider a vegetarian diet unhealthy because of the dependence on carbohydrates and processed protein-substitute foods to fill the gap left by meat and other animal-based foods.

While appealing to health seekers, vegetarianism comes with hazards—like vitamin B and protein deficiency—that must be prevented for a meat-free diet to be a healthy one.

Vegetarianism has benefits that are both global and health-related. But those who think vegetarianism is an easy, worry-free way to achieve better health would do well to consider some of the long-term implications of not eating meat, or, for vegans, any animal products. The challenges include getting enough protein and B vitamins in your diet, as well as ensuring that you don't go overboard on soy, processed foods, unhealthy sugars, and carbs. A vegetarian diet can be full of unexpected pitfalls if you're not prepared to work on getting balanced nutrition.

Possible Nutritional Deficiencies

Finding a good source of protein for each meal can be a challenge, at first, for vegetarians. Most North Americans are accustomed to having some form of meat at each meal, even when another high-protein food is present, yet for vegetarians it is these other sources of essential amino acids that are vital for a balanced diet. Without adequate amounts of each of the 9 essential amino acids, some vegetarians experience "brain fog," memory loss, tiredness, moodiness due to blood sugar highs and lows, lack of motivation, and poor performance at work or during exercise. Westerners living in enough relative wealth to contemplate vegetarianism as a lifestyle choice will almost never experience the kind of protein starvation that results in serious illnesses—but even slight protein deficiency can have a real impact on mental and physical health.

Iron and calcium are especially a concern for vegetarian women.

Similarly, vitamin B, iron, calcium, and other vitamins and minerals are a concern for vegans and vegetarians. Meat, eggs, and dairy are generally considered the best sources for these nutrients, some of which—such as B12—cannot be readily absorbed or processed in the human body from plant sources. (B12 is the most common nutritional deficiency in the developing world and possibly in the U.S., reports the *Harvard Health Letter*). For this reason, most vegetarians and particularly vegans must supplement their B vitamins, calcium, and iron or eat fortified foods like protein bars/powders, soy or rice milk, and cereals (which are, to varying degree, processed in ways that may be unhealthy—see below).

Iron and calcium are especially a concern for vegetarian women, who have to make up the iron lost monthly as blood hemoglobin during their period, and are more at risk than men of developing osteoporosis if their body's calcium needs are not sufficiently met.

If you are vegetarian and your body's need for protein, key vitamins, or minerals is not being met, one of the first warning signals may be a lack of energy—but a deficiency that makes one person feel listless and fatigued may have no effect on another. The amount of protein and vitamins needed can be highly individual. For this reason, it can be helpful to do some of your own research and discuss these issues with an expert nutritionist on vegan and vegetarian diets.

Reliance on Unhealthy Substitutes

One of the reasons that many health professionals consider a vegetarian diet unhealthy is the routine dependence on carbohydrates to fill the gap left by meat and other animal-based foods. Younger vegetarians are especially likely to lean on bread, cereal grains, sugary fruits, and desserts to fill them up while the rest of their family is eating meat or poultry, but adult vegetarians can fall prey to carbohydrate dependency and addiction as well. Foods rich in protein take longer for the body to digest and will fill you up, so a meal without enough protein will naturally leave a person hungry and can lead to overeating—usually of carbs. Excessive carbs and sugars become a vicious cycle, since eating sugar tends to make you crave more sweets. An unbalanced vegetarian diet without sufficient protein can lead to sugar addiction, blood sugar highs and lows, and in the long term even diabetes.

Other unhealthy vegetarian foods to watch out for include margarine (made of highly processed hydrogenated or partially hydrogenated fats; even "soft" non-hydrogenated margarine often contains toxic additives) and soy—which can be healthy in moderation, but dubious in large quantities since it can create hormone imbalances in both men and women. Heavily processed veg protein foods like textured soy protein, seitan, and fake meats (veggie dogs, veggie "chicken," "tofurkey," veggie slices) are good in extreme moderation but are very difficult for most people to digest because of their additives and the degree of processing they undergo.

Fortified rice/soy drinks and other foods that vegetarians are often directed towards can also be a mixed blessing. The sources of the vitamins and minerals in these foods are rarely listed and may be from natural or, more usually, from cheap manufactured sources that are difficult for the body to absorb and make use of—so you receive hardly any useable nutrition from them.

A vegetarian diet is, by definition, neither healthy nor unhealthy—like any diet, it depends on the extent of your knowledge and how much care you take to eat foods in balance, get the right nutrition for your body, and avoid overly processed foods and sugars. The website for VIVA, Vegetarians International Voice for Animals, summarizes nicely: "The truth is, most people who eat meat don't give a second thought to diet and nutrition and that's one of the reasons that diet-related illnesses such as obesity, diabetes and many cancers are on the increase." Vegetarianism comes with its own set of associated risks, but if you care enough to be a vegetarian, it's in your interest to give a second thought to your diet, take the time to get it right and do what's best for your health.

6

Vegetarian Diets Do Not Adversely Affect Athletes

Jonah Keri

Jonah Keri is a regular contributor to ESPN.com and the editor and co-author of the book Baseball Between the Numbers: Why Everything You Know About the Game Is Wrong.

Although it has not been proved that a vegetarian diet actually enhances an athlete's performance, many athletes believe vegetarianism does improve their stamina, mental alertness, ability to recover from injuries, and overall general health. There is some trial and error in learning about nutrition and developing the optimum balance of carbohydrates and proteins, but the effort is well worth it. Life is not just about sports; it is also about lifestyle and longevity.

With athletes paying more and more attention to what goes into their bodies and how nutrition affects performance, can a no-meat diet fuel success? Will more athletes turn to a meatless diet, whether for performance, or other reasons? How would such choices be received by a society that values meat eating and assumes our greatest athletes to be among the greatest carnivores? Because so many different factors affect performance, and all athletes have different bodies and metabolisms, how will we even know what's working and what isn't?

Already we've seen a number of world-class athletes move toward vegan and vegetarian diets. NBA [National Basketball

Association] guard Salim Stoudamire, former [National Football League] NFLers Desmond Howard and Ricky Williams, track and field greats Carl Lewis and Edwin Moses, and others have followed that path.... [O]ther athletes who have made the switch to vegan or vegetarian diets recently shared their thoughts on these and other meaty issues tied to their choices. Here's what they had to say:

The Football Player

When you're a Pro Bowl tight end, it's difficult to change your routine. Difficult, and maybe crazy. If you're in the midst of a Hall of Fame career, why change anything? As Tony Gonzalez [football player for the Kansas City Chiefs and Atlanta Falcons] discovered, sometimes change comes to you.

Sitting at home one day in May 2007, Gonzalez suddenly lost all feeling in his face and felt a terrible pain in the back of his head. He initially thought he was having a stroke, but hospital tests confirmed he had Bell's Palsy instead. Many doctors prescribe a diet consisting entirely of raw fruits, vegetables, nuts and seeds—no animal products or processed foods—as a way to improve digestion and combat the condition. A few months later, Gonzalez got another health scare, when doctors warned him of a low white blood cell count, raising the possibility he had leukemia. In the end, a mix-up with another patient's blood had caused that diagnosis. Still, with two scares in a span of a few months, Gonzalez became more attuned to his health and to what he put into his body.

Not long afterward, Gonzalez was on a cross-country flight when he struck up a conversation with the man next to him in first class. When lunchtime arrived, Gonzalez's seatmate ordered the salad with shrimp, hold the shrimp. Come dessert time, the man turned down the flight attendant's offer of milk to go with his cookies.

"So I asked him, 'Are you a vegetarian?'" Gonzalez recounted. "He said he was a vegan. Not eating meat I could understand, but I asked him why he wouldn't even drink the milk. He said that we're the only animals on Earth who drink milk after being babies."

A few years earlier, or maybe even a few months earlier, Gonzalez might have nodded politely and ended the conversation right there. But that year, he'd started to seriously ponder his long-term health and the dietary choices he was making. The health scares had opened his eyes. But more than that, Gonzalez wondered what life would be like after football. He wanted to stay in shape and live well after his playing days were done.

When the man recommended *The China Study* as a must read, Gonzalez devoured it. The 2005 book by Cornell professor and nutrition researcher T. Colin Campbell claims people who eat mostly plants contract fewer deadly diseases than those who eat mostly animals. The book got its name from diet studies and blood samples drawn from 6,500 men and women in China. Gonzalez has since met with Campbell and now plans to write his own book about dietary choices from the perspective of a 246-pound football star.

For Gonzalez, now 32, getting from Point A to Point B took a great deal of thought and self-doubt. Conventional wisdom held that eating steak and drinking a gallon of milk a day would make you big and strong and prepare you for the rigors of NFL life. Gonzalez followed that path, pounding steaks and milk, as well as pizza, hot dogs and burgers— whatever it took to pack on the pounds. He especially loved macaroni and cheese, with an emphasis on cheese, piled as high as possible. You couldn't argue with the results. In his first 10 seasons with the Kansas City Chiefs, Gonzalez had made the Pro Bowl eight times, establishing himself as the best tight end in the league.

The Right Balance

When he switched to a meatless diet, he wondered whether the move would backfire on him. At first, it looked like it might. In the first few weeks of his new regimen, he lost 10 pounds. His strength quickly dropped, and Gonzalez found himself unable to lift the heavy weights he'd hoisted with ease in the past. Teammates started telling him he looked skinny. "You're going to get your butt kicked" was another common refrain.

"It was a trial by error," he said. "I had to educate myself on how to do it the right way."

In the fourth quarters of games, he found himself sprinting past tired defenders.

After reading up on vegan-friendly recipes, Gonzalez found the right balance. Though he had more than enough money to buy any foods he wanted, Gonzalez still wasn't thrilled with the prospect of spending through the nose on groceries. Instead, his grocery bills stayed about the same, but the check at restaurants got slashed with no $50 porterhouse steaks on his plate. Gonzalez says he now focuses on produce when constructing his meals. He loads up on berries, bananas and mangoes, fresh vegetables and milk alternatives like rice milk or hemp milk, then blends them into what he calls "power smoothies."

He gained back most of his lost weight, settling in around 246 pounds. His strength quickly returned. When the season started, he was shocked at how good he felt. In the fourth quarters of games, he found himself sprinting past tired defenders. He became more alert during team meetings. On the day after a game, he'd skip into the gym, while teammates looked sore, beat up and worn out.

"People were still making fun of me, because I think they wanted to make themselves feel better," Gonzalez explained.

"I'd be ordering salad, potatoes, veggies. I think they felt guilty. Unless you've been in a cave, you know what's healthy and what's not healthy. But most of them still keep eating what they've been eating, because they think that's the only way to get enough protein and compete at a high level."

As the season progressed, Gonzalez's numbers picked up. Playing in his 11th season, Gonzalez made 99 catches (the second-highest total of his career), racking up 1,172 yards (the third-highest total of his career). In the previous three seasons, he'd dealt with an arthritic foot that got so bad he could barely walk the day after a game. The foot condition had forced him to give up basketball, a sport Gonzalez loved, having played varsity ball alongside the Sacramento Kings' Shareef Abdur-Rahim at Cal. Coincidence or not, the foot condition improved dramatically over the course of an offseason, to the point that he started hitting the hardwood again. Playing basketball in turn gave Gonzalez another good way to boost his training, which he says helped improve his agility.

More surprising than his improved health, he says, was the reaction of some of his friends, especially ex-players.

[M]aking the change was about living healthier and about recognizing there's a life beyond football.

Living Healthy

D'Marco Farr was a bruising NFL defensive lineman for seven seasons before injuries forced him into early retirement. Seven years after leaving the league, Farr told Gonzalez he still didn't feel 100 percent, carrying extra weight and still suffering from aches and pains. When Gonzalez told him about the changes he'd felt since going vegan, Farr jumped on board. He has since spread the word to other ex-players, including Lincoln Kennedy, a three-time Pro Bowler who retired at well more than 300 pounds.

Gonzalez has become something of a spokesman for healthy eating. When he retires, he wants to travel around the league speaking about the value of healthier diets. He's excited about the prospect of his first book on the subject. Gonzalez wants to reach out to younger players, too. He recently spoke to a group of 300 college football prospects at USC [University of Southern California], where he counseled the group not to fall into the trap of scarfing down fatty foods just because that's the norm for aspiring players trying to pack on weight.

"I believe in moderation," he said. "I know this isn't easy. One steak or a chicken dinner once in a while, that's fine. You just have to be smart about it. When you go from eating that way to a vegan diet, you can get into situations where it's like an alcoholic going to a bar: You say you're going to have one drink, and you end up having 10."

Pin Gonzalez down, and he'll concede his new diet hasn't necessarily improved his on-field performance. Science agrees with him on that point: No conclusive studies have proven a vegan or vegetarian diet helps an athlete run faster, jump higher or throw a ball harder or farther. To Gonzalez, making the change was about living healthier and about recognizing there's a life beyond football.

"In this league, you think you're invincible, that you'll last forever," he said. "Then you look at some of the numbers, that the average football player dies young. I'm sure there are other reasons, but eating unhealthy foods and carrying around all that extra weight can't help.

"I realized football's not going to last forever. To me this isn't a diet. It's a complete lifestyle change." . . .

The Ultramarathon Runner

Ultramarathon running is already tough enough. A typical race can cover 100 miles or more, often in scorching heat, blistering cold, or at dizzying elevation. As one of the leading ultramarathon runners in the world, Scott Jurek has had to deal with all of those challenges and more, vaulting scorpions in the desert, even meeting an occasional bear on the trails.

But Jurek adds another degree of difficulty to the mix. As a strict vegan, he goes through his grueling training regimen on a diet consisting of fruits, vegetables, grains and nuts. This seems completely impossible when you consider Jurek's typical calorie intake during peak training periods: 6,000 to 8,000 calories a day. Despite all that calorie loading, he packs just 165 pounds on his super lean, 6-foot-2 frame.

"For breakfast it's a dense, caloric smoothie," Jurek explained. "Then you've got lots of fruits and almonds. People assume it's all carbs. But there's also fat—avocados, rich mono-saturated fats, almonds, olive oil."

He's just getting warmed up.

"For protein you've got beans, lentils, combining whole grains. Tofu and tempeh. Then for carbs: whole grains, breads, cereals, fruits and veggies, whole foods, unprocessed foods. There's three main meals, then lots of smaller snack foods and mini-meals throughout the day."

Jurek's background didn't seem to portend a vegan diet years later. Born and raised in Minnesota, Jurek lived on meat and potatoes, regularly going out for hunting and fishing expeditions. After competing at Nordic skiing in his younger days, he ran his first ultramarathon in 1994.

As his ultramarathon career progressed, Jurek began phasing out meat from his diet. In 1999, Jurek read *Mad Cowboy*, the investigative book about the beef industry that prompted Oprah Winfrey to famously declare she'd never eat another burger. He became a vegetarian that year. Then, just before taking on the 100-mile Western States Endurance Run, he went vegan.

"I had my doubts, sure," Jurek recalled. "Am I going to be strong enough, have enough protein? There were all those common disclaimers, how it would affect my performance.

When I went on to win the race, I realized it was all just this mental barrier. After performing well on [the vegan diet], I never really doubted it afterwards."

Neither did Jurek's rivals. Not after he went on one of the most dominant runs in the history of his sport, including seven straight Western States victories. Instead, he often gets feedback from other distance runners, with everyone from beginners to high-level competitors telling Jurek that he inspires them to train harder and to seek out alternative diets.

[H]is diet does help him indirectly, in that it helps him recover from the pounding that his sport dishes out.

Still, Jurek says he never tries to impose his personal choices on anyone else. Nor does he see his vegan eating as a way to enhance performance. Like Danzig, Jurek says his diet does help him indirectly, in that it helps him recover from the pounding that his sport dishes out. A lot of people excel at ultramarathon running while living on unhealthy diets, he says.

"But where are they going to be in 20 years?" Jurek asked. "For me, it's about optimizing health. It's about lifestyle and longevity. Then you think about what vegetarian diets can do for the mass population, in terms of lower consumption of resources. When you look at the numbers, it's pretty staggering." . . .

7

Fad Diets Promote Unhealthy Eating Habits

Roberta Larson Duyff

Roberta Larson Duyff, award-winning author, national speaker, media writer, and food industry consultant, promotes the "power of positive nutrition." Duyff has authored several books including Nutrition and Wellness *(a high school text) and several children's healthy eating books.*

Fad diets, such as the grapefruit diet or high-fiber diet, may offer quick and easy weight loss, but the weight loss will usually be only temporary and can sometimes even damage health. For example, a high-protein diet may break down muscle, cause dehydration, and can be fatal for people with diabetes. The key to losing weight and keeping it off is to develop healthy eating habits and to eat a variety of foods. Fad diets promote just the opposite.

Every year Americans spend billions of dollars on the weight-loss industry—often for diet plans, diet books, services, and gimmicks that don't work! The lure of quick, easy weight loss is hard to resist, especially for those unwilling to make a commitment to lifelong behavioral change. Although the diets are ineffective in the long run, weight-loss hopefuls willingly give the next craze a chance. The result? Perhaps temporary results. But overall, wasted money, weight regained, a feeling of failure, and perhaps damage to health.

The next craze is often a past craze that's simply resurfaced with a new name, a new twist, yet still no sound science to back up the claims. Fad diets typically rely on nonscientific, unproved claims, personal stories, testimonials, or poorly controlled studies. Not surprisingly, many people feel confusion and diet fatigue as they sort through contradictory popular approaches to weight loss. Sound familiar? For those who try one fad diet after another, weight cycling becomes a common, frustrating problem. . . .

"Magical, One-Food" Diets

The "grapefruit diet," the "all-you-can-eat fruit diet," the "rice diet," "the cabbage soup diet," "the no dairy foods diet"! There's a weight-loss diet for almost every taste.

The facts are . . . Often touted to help melt fat away, no single-food or single-food-group diet has any special ability to do that. These diets don't work for several reasons. They lack variety. They don't provide adequate amounts of all the nutrients and protective phytonutrients the body needs for health, especially when some foods are off-limits. With unlimited quantities of "magical foods," the dieter runs the risk of overeating the foods featured on the so-called diet plan. Any weight loss—and lower calorie intake—comes from eliminating entire groups of other foods, not to any single food or food group.

The bottom line is that no super food can reverse weight gain resulting from inactivity and overeating. Eliminating a food or food category doesn't work either. Also, because these diets don't teach new eating habits, people usually don't stick with them!

Low-Carb, High-Protein Diets

Recent headlines and best-selling books promote low-carb and high-protein eating as a great solution to weight loss and fitness. Carbohydrate—starches and/or sugars—are often falsely accused as the culprits for weight gain. In fact, these diet plans aren't new. They've been around with different names for years.

The facts are . . . Simply because these diets are lower in calories, they may promote loss—if you stick with them. Here's what happens. By consuming fewer carbs, your body burns stored carbohydrates and releases water, thus water weight. If your carb intake is very low, your body also burns some fat, creating ketone bodies, which suppress appetite. If your total calorie intake (from any "energy nutrients") is low enough, you lose weight and muscle tissue.

A high-protein diet doesn't build muscle and burn fat, as some people think. Only regular physical activity and training build muscle strength and burn calories stored in body fat.

Because these weight loss plans are common today, research is under way looking at low to moderate carbohydrate diets for weight loss. They may be appropriate for some people, perhaps those with insulin resistance. Stay tuned. . . . A moderate-carbohydrate diet with more protein may help some people lose body fat while maintaining muscle as they lose weight.

For most people, a low-carbohydrate, high-protein eating approach for weight loss raises concerns:

- These diets do promote rapid weight loss—at first. Their diuretic effect promotes loss of water weight, not body fat, however. The psychological lift offers a false sense of success that's quickly gone when water weight returns.

- Depending on the foods consumed, a high-protein, low-carb diet may be high in total fat, saturated fat, and cholesterol. Inconsistent with sound nutrition advice, this weight loss regimen over time can increase the risk for heart disease and perhaps some forms of cancer.

- A diet that restricts many starchy foods is often low in fiber. The possible result? Constipation and other gastrointestinal disorders. A low-fiber diet isn't consistent with guidelines for health.

- A condition called ketosis (increased blood ketones from incomplete fat breakdown) can result with these regimens. Ketosis suppresses hunger and thus contributes to lower calorie intake. Some popular diets claim that ketosis hastens weight loss. In truth, muscle also breaks down due to a lack of carbohydrate for energy. In addition, ketosis can cause weakness nausea, dehydration, light-headedness, and irritability. It can be fatal to people with diabetes, and during pregnancy may cause birth defects or fetal death.

High-Fiber, Low-Calorie Diets

The flip side of the high-protein craze may be the high-fiber approach to dieting. It's true that most of us need more fiber to promote good health. Depending on your age and gender, 25 to 38 grams of fiber a day are advised for adults. . . . Too much—perhaps resulting from fiber a day are supplements—may be too much of a good thing!

The facts are . . . As a food component, fiber isn't absorbed, so it doesn't contribute calories. That's why high-fiber foods such as whole grains, vegetables, legumes, and fruits—usually lower in calories—are included in weight-loss diets. These diets are quite filling, so you might eat less overall.

Very-high-fiber diets may come up short on protein foods. And they can cause constipation and dehydration if extra fluids aren't consumed.

Bulk fillers, which are high in fiber, aren't advised. They reduce hunger by first absorbing liquid, then swelling up in the stomach. These products can be harmful when they obstruct the digestive tract. . . .

Eating enough fiber-rich foods, as part of a healthful weight-loss plan, is a smarter idea!

Very-Low-Calorie Liquid Diets

Very-low-calorie liquid formulas have been developed for short-term use under a doctor's supervision. To help some obese people, they may aid short-term weight loss—if there's also a commitment to new eating and active living habits. Used as a liquid diet without other foods, they're very low in calories, providing just 400 to 800 calories a day.

These formulas were changed after deaths were attributed to their use. Newer formulas have more vitamins, minerals, and high-quality protein.

The facts are . . . Without medical supervision and nutrition education, liquid diets don't teach new ways of eating. Since people usually don't stay with them, there's usually no long-term weight loss. They also may result in fatigue, constipation, nausea, diarrhea, or hair loss. For people with some health problems, such as insulin-dependent diabetes or kidney disease, a very-low-calorie liquid diet can be harmful.

Fasting

As a tactic, does fasting jump-start weight loss?

The facts are . . . As with very-low-calorie diets, fasting deprives the body of energy and nutrients needed for normal functions. Any rapid weight loss is mostly water and muscle loss. Fasting also may cause fatigue and dizziness, with less energy for physical activity. And it feeds the cycle of "yo-yo" dieting.

As an aside, there's a misconception that fasting "cleans out" the system, removing toxic wastes. To the contrary, body chemicals called ketones build up in the body when carbohydrates aren't available for energy. Ketosis puts a burden on the kidneys; as noted, ketones that accumulate can be harmful to health.

Gimmicks, Gadgets, and Other "Miracles"

Promoters advertise "easy ways to weight loss"—weight-loss patches, electric muscle stimulators, spirulina (a species of blue-green algae), starch and fat blockers, creams that melt fat away, and many others. . . .

The facts are . . . All these products have been offered for sale and purport to promote weight loss. Yet none proves effective. Some even may be harmful. And they're all a waste of money!

The popular press often advertises massages and other therapies for losing "cellulite," dimpled fat on thighs and hips. Cellulite is simply normal body fat under the skin that looks lumpy when the fat layer gets thick, allowing connective, fibrous-looking tissue that holds fat in place to show. The lumpy look can lessen or disappear with normal weight loss.

You've probably seen weight-loss programs that sweat off extra weight. Sweating in a sauna—or wearing a rubber belt or nylon clothes that make you perspire during exercise—may cause weight loss. However, the pounds that disappear are water loss, not body fat. When you drink or eat, weight returns.

Instead of helping to achieve a healthful weight goal, "sweating off" pounds may damage health through dehydration. . . .

8

Fat Acceptance Promotes Well-Being

Elizabeth Sutherland

Elizabeth Sutherland is a teacher and writer from Melbourne, Australia. She is the author of the blog Spilt Milk, *in which she writes mainly about feminist motherhood and fat activism.*

Today's culture of dieting to obtain the ideal body promotes shame and degradation. From mothers who critique their children's body parts, and publications that airbrush photographs to showcase the "perfect" bodies of models and celebrities, to the diet industry that bombards the public with scorn over love handles and belly rolls—it is all about hurt. Today's culture needs to change to one that promotes kindness and positive regard for people, no matter what shape or size.

Once, when I was in my late teens, I had a fleeting reunion with my mother, with whom I'd had very little contact since childhood. It had been about five years since we'd seen each other in person; I was apprehensive about our meeting but mostly I was excited. Fantasies about happy mother-daughter bonding even after such a long estrangement are really *that* seductive. She did me a favour though and squashed them right away with her greeting: where I had imagined tearful embraces and a tumble of words was simply "My gosh, you've gotten fat! I was never that fat in my life, you know." Evidently I'd smooshed her happy families fantasy too—I wasn't the daughter she'd ordered. I was kind of shameful.

Body Shame

I'm aware that my little anecdote is not typical (my mother is ill and we've never had a 'normal' relationship). But I also know that some version of body-shaming goes on in most families. Mothers sitting around prodding their own cellulite and reprimanding themselves for eating a slice of cake condition their children to think it's normal to hate their bodies. We know this so well it's practically a cliché. It's also a familiar kind of mother-blaming: someone develops an eating disorder, and everyone starts asking questions of the mother. Publications wanting to promote a fuzzy ideal of healthy body image may typically devote column inches to admonishing mothers for engaging in diet culture in front of their daughters. These sit nicely alongside narratives about neglectful mothers lazily ordering take-away and overbearing mothers plumping up their children with too much sugary love and fatty indulgence. Hence, I'm wary of the misogyny lurking behind critiques of mothers' behaviour towards their bodies and food. Whilst it's a goal of feminism to allow for the dissection and transgression of narrow beauty ideals, it's clearly not feminist to lay the blame for the perpetuation of young people's low self esteem upon women in the way that popular narratives about mothers and daughters often seem to do.

Still, there's a kernel of truth in there. I do wonder how my own relationship with my body may have been different had my mother been kinder to me. Body shame is a great tool of kyriarchy [the structure of power within a society] and we often get it from our mothers first, as we learn how bodies can be reduced to a collection of parts and how those parts can be ranked in order of acceptability. Thighs and bums, boobs and upper arms, back-fat and belly-rolls can all be prodded and critiqued, despaired over, disparaged, loathed. This is often a social activity, too. Who doesn't love normalising misogyny over a cup of tea and a (low calorie) biscuit while the kids play in the next room?

Me, actually. I don't love it.

Body Acceptance

I'm fat (a lot fatter now than the 200lbs or so that so offended my mother way back then). My body is relatively healthy (I'm not going to delve into the 'but fat is so unhealthy!' quagmire here: that swamp's been negotiated by others far more intrepid than me). It's also the body that conceived and carried and birthed and fed my daughter. It's the body that takes me through my days. It's the body *that is me*. I accept it and love it because accepting and loving myself in this world that wants to tell me that I ought to be ashamed is an act of rebellion. Every time I choose to be kind to myself I'm advocating for fat acceptance.

> *Jumping off the weight loss merry-go-round . . . is not only brave and radical but it's joyous and positive, too.*

Each moment that we choose to be kind to others by approaching them with unconditional positive regard, whatever their size or shape, we are activists. Doing this kicks back at a culture of fear and shame surrounding our bodies.

Not only are we bombarded each day with impossibly airbrushed photographs of 'perfect' models and other celebrities, but we see plenty of the alternative. We see the headless fatties in the news reports, the women who loathe themselves in the breast cancer campaigns, and women who make an art out of self-deprecation in sit-coms and diet ads. The unhappy, waist-minding, calorie-counting, love-handle pinching woman is such a common trope that we barely notice her anymore. Characters like Bridget Jones make it endearing to be cruel to oneself and apparently, audiences have lapped that shit right up.

The diet industry can't survive if we don't loathe ourselves. Jumping off the weight loss merry-go-round isn't about giving up hope or about giving in to weakness. To the contrary, choosing to inhabit space outside of the dominant discourses about weight, as fat activists do, is not only brave and radical but it's joyous and positive, too. And it should be possible for everyone.

Some people don't like the term fat acceptance. Acceptance can sound too close to tolerance (oh well if you *must* be fat all over the place, I suppose that's your prerogative). To others, acceptance can seem too much like resignation. Referring to what size acceptance advocates do as 'fat activism' instead may give more weight (har har) to it as a social justice movement, may lend a more positive and active spin. Perhaps that is true.

Changing the Rules

To me, though, acceptance is perfect. Acceptance is not giving up—it's changing the rules.

Diet culture, even when it doesn't involve surgeries or starvation or physical harm (although it very often does involve these things) is violence. Even the language of diet culture is about hurt: *burn those calories, zap that fat, I've been so bad, no pain no gain, beat the hunger, crush the cravings, fight the fat, battle the bulge, waging war on obesity.* See? All about the hurt. It's no wonder then that some people seem to perceive fat acceptance as a new kind of danger. Some assume it's a movement that promotes harm to one's own body or to the health of others, or even to taxpayers. It doesn't. It simply illuminates this fact: if there is a war on obesity, there's a war on 'obese people' and those people have a right to resist. So we do, often by opting out of the war altogether and making peace with bodies. I don't want to fight my body anymore and I sure as hell don't want to fight yours, whatever size it is. In fact, I don't even want all that rhetoric about fighting. Why are softer words (embrace, accept, listen) less utilized? Traits commonly seen as 'feminine' and therefore weak—like kindness—are actually some of the most effective mechanisms we have to use against fat-hate. It's hard to sell diet pills to someone who'd like to be gentle on themselves, accept themselves for who they are, listen to what their body needs and embrace size diversity. And it's hard to see how creating a world without diet pills wouldn't be a win for feminism.

Acceptance is not giving up—it's changing the rules.

Not fighting isn't necessarily surrender. It could mean being the mother who doesn't dissect and grade her body parts in front of her children. Or, as the brilliant Charlotte Cooper reportedly said at the recent Fat Studies conference in Sydney [Australia], 'fat activism can be as simple as walking down the street eating an ice cream.' Maybe it's walking with someone you care about, while they eat that ice cream. Gazing in the mirror and knowing that your cellulite is not a moral failing is activism (and feminism). Asking your friends to shift their focus off of your weight and onto your well-being is activism. Insisting that the bodily autonomy of everyone, no matter what size, should be honoured, is activism. And telling your doctor that you want to follow a Health At Every Size approach to health, and why? Activism.

Sometimes fat acceptance is just choosing to cut the snark and show some respect to the human body in its diverse awesomeness. A little kindness—*just kindness*—is one of the most powerful forms of feminist activism available to us. We should use it.

9

Fasting and Juice Cleansing Can Heal the Body

Elson M. Haas

Elson M. Haas is the founder and director of the Preventive Medical Center of Marin in San Rafael, California. He is the author of several health and nutrition books, including The New Detox Diet, Staying Healthy with the Seasons, *and* The False Fat Diet.

Fasting to heal the body is instinctively used by animals and has been used for thousands of years by many religious followers to purify the body and attain spiritual enlightenment. Many people today eat an acid-forming diet consisting of too much protein, fat, sugar, and chemicals and not enough essential vitamins and minerals. Juice fasting is an excellent way to rest the gastro-intestinal tract, let the cells and tissues repair themselves, and clear out the diseased cells and toxins that can cause degeneration and sickness.

Fasting is the single greatest natural healing therapy I know. It is nature's ancient, universal remedy for many problems, used instinctively by animals when they are ill and by earlier cultures for healing and spiritual purification. When I first discovered fasting 30 years ago, I felt as if it had saved my life. With my first fast, my stagnant energies began flowing, my allergies, aches, and pains disappeared, and I became more creative and vitally alive. I still find fasting both a useful personal tool and an important therapy for many medical and life problems.

Most of the conditions for which I recommend fasting are ones that result from excess nutrition rather than undernourishment. Dietary abuses generate many chronic degenerative diseases (such as atherosclerosis, hypertension, heart disease, allergies, diabetes, cancer, and substance abuse) that undermine our health and precede body's breakdown. Fasting is not only therapeutic, but, more important, it acts in preventing many conditions. It often becomes the catalyst for shifting from unhealthy or abusive habits to a more healthful lifestyle in general. As I use the term here, *fasting* refers to the avoidance of solid food and the intake of liquids only. True fasting would be the total avoidance of anything by mouth. The most stringent form of fasting allows drinking water exclusively; more liberal fasting includes the juices of fresh fruit and vegetables as well as herbal teas. All of these methods generate a high degree of detoxification. Individual experiences with fasting depend on the overall condition of the body, mind, and attitude. Detoxification can be intense and may either temporarily increase sickness or be immediately helpful and uplifting.

Promotes Rejuvenation

Juice fasting is commonly used (rather than water alone) as a mild and effective cleansing plan. Fresh juices are easily assimilated and require minimum digestion, while they supply many nutrients and stimulate the body to clear its wastes. Juice fasting is also safer than water fasting, because it supports the body nutritionally while cleansing and probably even produces a better detoxification and quicker recovery. Fasting (cleansing, detoxification) is 1 part of the trilogy of nutrition; balancing and building (toning) are the others. I believe that fasting is the missing link in the Western diet and lifestyle. And juice cleansing is a true therapeutic program. Most people overeat, eat too often, and eat a high-protein, high-fat, acid-forming, and congesting diet more consistently than is necessary. When we regularly eat a balanced, well-combined, more alkalinizing diet, we will have less need for fasting and toning plans (although both are still highly beneficial, performed throughout the year).

Fasting is not only therapeutic, but more important, it acts in preventing many conditions.

Detoxification is a time when we allow our cells and organs to breathe and restore themselves; it can be a time of rejuvenation. However, we do not necessarily need to fast to experience some cleansing. Even minor dietary shifts—including an increase in fluids, more raw foods, and fewer congesting foods—will initiate and promote better bodily function and improved detoxification. For example, a vegetarian or macrobiotic diet will be cleansing and purifying to someone on a heavier diet. Fasting is a time-proven remedy, with human origins going back many thousands of years. Voluntary abstinence from food has been a tradition in most religions and is still used as a spiritual purification rite. Such religions as Christianity, Judaism, Islam, Buddhism, and Hinduism have encouraged fasting as penance, preparation for ceremony, purification, mourning, sacrifice, divine union, and to enhance mental and spiritual powers. The Bible is filled with stories of people fasting for purification and communion with God. The Essenes, authors of the Dead Sea Scrolls, also advocated fasting as a primary method of healing and spiritual revelation, as described in the *Essene Gospel of Peace* (translated by Edmond Bordeaux Szekely from the third-century Aramaic manuscript). . . .

From a medical point of view, I believe that fasting is not used often enough. We take vacations from work to relax, recharge, and gain new perspectives on our life—why not take occasional breaks from food? (Or, for that matter, from excessive activity or television and other electronics?) To break the habit of eating three meals a day is a challenge for most of us. When we stop and let our stomach remain empty, the body goes into an elimination cycle, and most people will experience some withdrawal symptoms, especially when toxicity exists. Symptoms include headaches, irritability, and fatigue. As with all allergy-addictions, eating again assuages these symptoms.

Fasting Alleviates Many Ailments

Fasting is a useful therapy for so many conditions and people. Those who tend to develop congestive symptoms do well with fasting; congestive acidic conditions include colds, flus, bronchitis, mucus congestion, and constipation. . . . If not addressed, such conditions can lead to headaches, chronic intestinal problems, skin conditions, and more severe ailments. Most of us living in Western, industrialized nations suffer from both overnutrition and undernutrition. We take in excessive amounts of potentially toxic nutrients, such as fats, sugars, and chemicals, and inadequate amounts of many essential vitamins and minerals. The resulting congestive diseases are characterized by excess mucus and sluggish elimination; deficiency problems result from either poor nourishment or ineffective digestion and assimilation. Juice fasting supplies nutrients while still allowing for the elimination of toxins.

The general detoxification and cleansing program discussed a number of symptoms and diseases of toxicity that can be alleviated by detoxification. Juice fasting is mentioned as part of the treatment plans for many other programs. It can be used to detoxify from drugs or whenever we want to embark on a new plan or life transition, provided that there are no contraindications to fasting. Short-term fasting is versatile and generally fairly safe; however, when it is used in the treatment of medical conditions, proper supervision should be employed, including monitoring of physical changes and biochemistry values. Many doctors, clinics, acupuncturists, nutritionists, and chiropractors feel comfortable overseeing people during cleansing and detox programs, and I encourage you to seek them out if your condition warrants supervision.

The use of fasting as a treatment for fevers is controversial, but it should not be. Consuming liquids generates less heat, which helps to cool the body. With fever, we need more liquids than usual. Some cases of fatigue respond well to fasting, particularly when the fatigue results from congested organs and stalled energy. With fatigue that results from chronic infection, nutritional deficiency, or serious disease, added nourishment is probably called for as opposed to fasting.

Back pain caused by muscular tightness and stress (rather than from bone disease or osteoporosis) is usually alleviated with a lighter diet or juice fasting. Much tightness and soreness along the back results from colon or other organ congestion; in my experience, poor bowel function and constipation are commonly associated with back pain.

[A] short 5- to 10-day fast can motivate people to make the necessary dietary changes and renewed commitments to proper eating.

Patients with mental illness ranging from anxiety to schizophrenia may be helped by fasting. Although this may sound sensational, fasting's purpose here is not to cure these problems but rather to help understand the relationship of foods, chemicals, and drugs with mental functioning. Additional allergies and environmental reactions are not at all uncommon in people with mental illness. True, the release of toxins or lack of nourishment during fasting may worsen psychiatric problems; if, however, the patient is strong and congested, fasting may be helpful. The supervision of a health-care provider is important for patients with mental illness.

People often attempt to remedy obesity by fasting, although it is not the best use of this healing technique. Fasting is actually too temporary an approach for overweight dieters and may even generate feasting reactions in people coming off the fast. A better solution would be a more gradual change of diet with a longer-term weight-reduction plan—something that will replace old dietary habits and food choices with new ones. However, a short 5- to 10-day fast can motivate people to make the necessary dietary changes and renewed commitments to proper eating. . . .

Fasting increases the process of elimination and the release of toxins from the colon, kidneys and bladder, lungs and sinuses, and skin. This process can generate discharge such as mucus from the gastrointestinal tract, respiratory tract, sinuses, or in the urine. This is helpful to clear out the problems that have arisen from overeating and a sedentary lifestyle. Much of aging and disease, I believe, results from biochemical suffocation, where the cells do not get enough oxygen and nutrients or cannot adequately eliminate their wastes. Fasting helps us decrease this suffocation by allowing the cells to eliminate and catch up with current processes.

Fasting Transforms the Body, Mind, and Emotions

This physiological rest and concentration on cleanup can also generate a number of toxicity symptoms. Hunger is usually present for 2 or 3 days and then departs, leaving many people with a surprising feeling of deep abdominal peace; yet others may feel really hungry. It is good to ask ourselves, "What am I hungry for?" Fasting is an excellent time to work on our psychological connections to consumption. . . .

Nutritionally, fasting helps us appreciate the more subtle aspects of our diet, as less food and simple flavors will become more satisfying (even food aromas can be fulfilling). Mentally, fasting improves clarity and attentiveness; emotionally, it may make us more sensitive and aware of our feelings. I have seen individuals gain the clarity to make important decisions during this therapy, particularly regarding jobs and relationships. Fasting definitely supports the transformational, evolutionary process. Juice fasting offers a lesson in self-restraint and control of passions. This new and empowering sense of self-discipline can be highly motivating. Fasters who were once spectators suddenly become doers. Fasting is a simple process of self-cleansing. We do not need any special medicines to do it; our body knows how. Provided that we are basically well nourished, systematic undereating and fasting are likely the most important contributors to health and longevity. Fasting is even more important to balance the autointoxication that results from common dietary and drug indiscretions.

Fasting increases the process of elimination and the release of toxins. . . .

I look at fasting as taking a week off work to handle the other aspects of life for which there is often little time. With fasting we can take time to nurture ourselves and rest. Fasting is also like turning off and cleaning a complex and valuable machine so that it will function better and longer. Resting the gastro-intestinal tract, letting the cells and tissues repair themselves, and allowing the lymph, blood, and organs to clear out old, defective, or diseased cells and unneeded chemicals all lead to less degeneration and sickness. As healthy cell growth is stimulated, so is our level of vitality, immune function, and disease resistance as well as our potential for greater longevity. . . .

Fasting Creates Some Risk

If fasting is overused, it may create depletion and weakness in the body, lowering resistance and increasing susceptibility to disease. Although fasting does allow the organs, tissues, and cells to rest and handle excesses, the body needs the nourishment provided by food to function after it has used up its stores. Malnourished people should definitely not fast, nor should some overweight people who are undernourished. Others who should not fast include people with fatigue resulting from nutrient deficiency, those with chronic degenerative disease of the muscles or bones, or those who are underweight. Diseases associated with clogged or toxic organs respond better to fasting. Sluggish individuals who retain water or whose weight is concentrated in their hips and legs often do worse. Those with low daytime energy and more vitality at night (more yin or alkaline types) may not enjoy fasting either.

Fasting is also like turning off and cleaning a complex and valuable machine so that it will function better and longer.

I do not recommend fasting for pregnant or lactating women, or for people who have weak hearts, or weakened immunity. (I have, however, seen women use short juice cleanses during their menstrual cycle to help ease pain and other symptoms.) Before or after surgery is not a good time to fast, as the body needs its nourishment to handle the stress and healing demands of the operation. Although some nutritional therapies for cancer include medically supervised fasting, I do not recommend it for cancer patients, particularly those with advanced problems. Ulcer disease is not something for which I usually suggest fasting, either, although fasting may be beneficial for other conditions present in a patient whose ulcer is under control. . . .

Fasting Is Nature's Tool

Fasting can easily become a way of life and an effective dietary practice. Over a period of time we can go from symptom cleansing to preventive fasting. We should support ourselves regularly with a balanced, wholesome diet, and fast at specific times to treat symptoms and/or to enhance our vitality and spiritual practice. If we could devote one day a week to purification and a cleansing diet, the path of health would be smooth indeed. . . . We all overdo it with foods or other substances at different times and then may need fasting more frequently. We all need to return to the cycle of a daily fast of 12 to 14 hours overnight until our morning "break fast" and then find our own natural pattern of food consumption. This usually means one main meal and two lighter ones. For low-weight, high-metabolism people, two larger or three moderately sized meals are probably needed. If we eat a heavier evening meal, we need only a light breakfast, and vice versa. Through awareness and experience, we can find our individual nutritional needs and fulfill them by listening to that inner nutritionist—the body.

Choosing healthy foods, chewing well, and maintaining good colon function all minimize the need for fasting. However, if we do get out of balance, we can employ one of the oldest treatments known to humans, the instinctive therapy for many illnesses, Nature's doctor, therapist, and tool for preventing disease—FASTING!

10

Broad Eating Patterns
Are Healthier
than Restrictive Diets

Katherine Hobson

Katherine Hobson is a senior writer for U.S. News & World Report *and has appeared on NBC's the* Today Show, *CNN, MSNBC, and CBS, as well as on numerous other radio and television outlets.*

Instead of trying to isolate a single vitamin or nutrient, like Vitamin C or beta carotene, nutrition scientists should focus on a whole diet pattern taken together to promote health and protect against disease. For example, the Mediterranean eating pattern (which includes more fruits, vegetables, olive oil, and less red meat than the current Westernized diet) leads to healthier people, yet no one knows exactly why. It could be the way the foods work together, or it could be because certain foods are left out. Whatever the answer, the key to a healthy diet plan is to eat good-quality wholesome foods on a regular basis and not depend on a single "superfood" or nutritional supplement.

Earlier this year [2008], the "Mediterranean diet" turned 15. Of course, for the people who actually live in the Mediterranean region, that's an absurd notion. They have been eating meals of fish, vegetables, and whole grains drizzled with olive oil, then washing it all down with a glass or two of wine for generations. What actually turned 15 is the Mediterranean

Diet Pyramid, an attempt by nutrition experts to promote an alternative to the typical overprocessed, fat- and sugar-laden American diet.

That pyramid—like other recently devised dietary guides built on age-old traditions—represents a way of looking at nutrition that's gathering steam these days. Rather than reducing a diet to its essential foods and then foods to their essential nutrients—vitamins, minerals, and other chemicals—and trying to isolate those that may contribute to good health, researchers are increasingly taking a step back and correlating health with broader eating patterns. "What we're talking about is the background diet," says Linda Van Horn, acting chair of preventive medicine at Northwestern University's Feinberg School of Medicine. "It's not the occasional hot fudge sundae or brownie; rather, it's the day-to-day, meal-to-meal, bite-to-bite: What is it that appears in your mouth?"

Looking at the Whole Diet—Not a Single Element

The focus is on finding the overall combination of foods that are associated with better health, without necessarily pinpointing individual elements of the diet that are responsible. That may involve studying how people in different areas of the world eat or, here at home, using statistics to study which foods the healthiest among us consume. "You find out who's healthy, then ask what they're eating and how much they exercise," says K. Dun Gifford, founder and president of Oldways Preservation Trust, the Boston-based food issues think tank that developed the Mediterranean Diet Pyramid. (More later on the exercise element, which often gets lost when people try to adopt a healthier diet.)

Oldways, which gets funding from food companies and trade associations, among others, and developed its recommendations in conjunction with the Harvard School of Public Health, has also created food pyramids for a traditional healthful Asian diet, which emphasizes vegetables such as bok choy and chilies, noodles, and beans, as well as a traditional Latin American diet. The group has also cooked up a healthful vegetarian pyramid; plant-based diets, when they include all the essential nutrients, are associated with low rates of chronic diseases and longevity.

The focus is on finding the overall combination of foods that are associated with better health. . . .

It's important to recognize the flaws in the old-fashioned approach to nutrition science, which is to search for the precise health-promoting vitamin or chemical in a food and then to isolate it. That often results in taking wonder ingredient X out of the food entirely and putting it into a pill or into foods it was never meant to be in (think orange juice spiked with the omega-3 fatty acids naturally found in fish). That kind of ingredient isolation and supplementation was appropriate when many people suffered from diseases caused by a lack of a certain nutrient, like scurvy (vitamin C) or rickets (vitamin D). Those problems could easily be fixed by adding back the missing piece. "But there's a big difference between deficiency diseases and chronic diseases, where it's more likely that there are multiple factors acting in concert," says Marion Nestle, a nutritionist at New York University and author of, most recently, *What to Eat.* "It's hard, in that situation, to tease out the role of a single nutrient."

Not that people haven't tried. Consider the health claims for various vitamins, minerals, and other nutrients over the years. Vitamin A and C, which are antioxidants, and carotenoids like beta carotene and lycopene were once touted as tools to fight chronic diseases like cancer. It was a logical hypothesis; people who eat a lot of fruits and veggies are healthier than those who don't. Shouldn't the chemicals that are unique to these foods be responsible? As it turns out, no.

"The history has been that the first studies [to test individual nutrients] show fabulous benefits, and then as they were repeated with larger populations, better placebos, and better controls, not only were they not helping, but in some cases they may hurt," says Nestle. The poster child is beta carotene, which not only didn't stave off lung cancer but actually appeared to increase rates of the disease among smokers. (A similar outcome was reported earlier this year with vitamin E.) Now we're back to where we started: Fruits and veggies appear to be protective, but we still don't know why.

Soy was also considered as a miracle food. When Japanese people move to the West, for example, their rates of chronic diseases like diabetes and heart disease go up. Researchers naturally wondered whether missing dietary elements might be responsible. They realized that these immigrants largely gave up soy for other protein sources, so the researchers focused on isoflavonoids, a group of chemicals found mostly in soy and suspected of guarding against chronic disease, says Christopher Gardner, a nutrition scientist at the Stanford Prevention Research Center. Again, a logical assumption didn't pan out in larger studies.

But what if it's not a single chemical or food that traditionally protected the Japanese, says Gardner, but how all components of their diet interact? "Maybe it's not just the tofu but the tofu in the stir fry with the sesame oil," he says. "The frustrating thing in nutrition is that for the last couple of decades, so many studies have failed because we've isolated one nutrient at a time, when probably the benefit comes from the synergistic and additive effects of the whole diet taken together."

Studying the Mediterranean Eating Pattern

Having in a sense returned to the drawing board, researchers are increasingly looking at those conventional patterns of eating as models for healthful eating. Dietary patterns are most easily described by their ethnic origins. "Low-carb or low-fat diets are a man-made phenomenon," says Van Horn. "Instead, what we're talking about is the more cultural, traditional, historical eating pattern—like the Mediterranean diet."

That's the dietary tradition with the most evidence behind it; scientists have been studying Mediterranean eating patterns and their impact on health since after World War II, when diet was suspected to account for the remarkable health of people living on Crete. Since then, research has associated the Mediterranean way of eating with a host of health benefits, including protection against diabetes, cancer, and heart disease.

Of course, there's a high degree of variability among the dietary traditions that encompass the Mediterranean, says Judith Wylie-Rosett, head of behavioral and nutrition research at the Albert Einstein College of Medicine in New York. The same is true of Asian and Latin American diets. But pretty much any traditional diet is better than our current westernized diet, which is, by all accounts, a mess. "The public-health crisis we are facing is a direct result of the western diet: lots of refined, processed, and manufactured food, lots of red meat, lots of added fat and sugar, very little whole grains or fruits and vegetables," says Michael Pollan, whose latest book, *In Defense of Food*, lays out the case for a holistic approach to eating.

"[W]hat we're talking about is the more cultural, traditional, historical eating pattern." . . .

So some nutritionists are taking a stab at more precisely describing dietary patterns, using statistical analysis to measure what foods tend to cluster together in the diets of healthy (or not healthy) people. For example, a "prudent" eating pattern is characterized by higher intakes of fruit, vegetables, whole grains, legumes, and fish, says Teresa Fung, a nutritionist at Simmons College in Boston. That pattern has been shown to be associated with a lower risk of coronary heart disease, type 2 diabetes, and colorectal cancer, as well as lower body mass index.

The prudent diet has some key similarities with most of the ethnic eating patterns. "A better diet, however you define it, almost always includes more fruits and vegetables, less processed meat, more whole grains, fish, nuts, and low-fat dairy," says Katherine Tucker, a nutritional epidemiologist at Tufts University's Friedman School of Nutrition Science and Policy.

The key is replacing less healthful foods with healthier ones. . . .

The beauty of the pattern approach is that it's not necessary to know exactly what mechanism is leading to better health. "It could be one thing or multiple things," says Fung. For example, research recently suggested that the higher amounts of choline, an essential nutrient in the vitamin B family, and another nutrient called betaine—both of which are abundant in a Mediterranean diet—reduce inflammation, which may contribute to a host of diseases, says Steven Zeisel, director of the Nutrition Research Institute at Kannapolis, a branch of the UNC [University of North Carolina] Chapel Hill School of Public Health. "But the truth is, I'd be foolish to rush out and eat those nutrients. I can eat closer to that pattern—less red meat, more olive oil—and not worry about which is the active ingredient," he says. In fact, it's not even clear that these patterns are healthier because of what's in them—it may be what's absent. "As soon as you eat the Mediterranean diet, you're eating less steak," says Gardner. "Maybe it had nothing to do with that. What we know is that if you eat that way, you're healthier."

Incorporating Exercise Along with Wholesome Foods

So, is it that easy: We all just have to eat like the Greeks (or the Vietnamese, or the ancient Maya)? Well, yes and no. First, most of the evidence comes from observation, not rigorous scientific trials, so it doesn't prove cause and effect. But there's enough observational data to convince most researchers, and there is some experimental evidence: Trials showed that eating a low-sodium diet based on whole grains, poultry, fish, and nuts and lighter on the red meat, fats, and sweets lowered blood pressure.

A second caveat is that these ancient dietary patterns were long paired with a way of life that doesn't much exist in America—and it included a lot of exercise, says Pollan. Men in postwar Crete didn't laze around dunking bread in olive oil all day; they chased goats up hills. Even now, people in the Mediterranean and other parts of the world are more active, whether through vocation or because there's so much more walking as part of daily life. That's why the traditional food pyramids from Oldways all include exercise. (The government recommends 30 minutes a day of moderate exercise for heart health and 60 to 90 minutes a day for weight loss.)

And if you're watching your weight—and who isn't?—calories really do count. The key is replacing less healthful foods with healthier ones, not just adding tofu to your bologna sandwich or nuts to your sundae. As Pollan says, "Eat food. Not too much. Mostly plants." That doesn't mean eschewing all indulgences, but it does mean keeping an eye on day-to-day intake. "It's about the pattern over the long term," says Oldways' Gifford. "Do you think people in the Mediterranean get drunk after church on Sunday? Sure, they do! We're human, and you have to take the pressure off the pressure cooker."

Even with occasional excesses, adopting a sound dietary pattern may be both simpler and more wholesome than chasing down the latest superfood or nutritional supplement. "Finally, the field has come around to realize that it won't be a single nutrient," says Tucker. "We're back to old-fashioned advice: Eat a variety of good-quality whole foods. That's the way to stay optimally healthy."

11

The Emphasis on Dieting Harms Girls

Jeffrey Zaslow

Jeffrey Zaslow is a columnist for the Wall Street Journal *and the author or coauther of three bestselling books,* The Last Lecture, The Girls from Ames, *and* Highest Duty.

In 1986, 100 nine-year-old girls were asked how they felt about their bodies, and 75 percent thought they weighed too much. Over twenty years later, many of those same girls were interviewed again and said that, over the years, they have continued to diet and battle with self-esteem issues. In fact, researchers believe that society's obsession with slimness has gotten even more pressure-packed, so much so that disordered eating patterns, such as bulimia and anorexia, are showing up in children as young as age five.

One day in January 1986, fourth-grade girls at Marie Murphy School in Wilmette, Ill., were called down to the principal's office.

A stranger was waiting there to ask each girl a question: "Are you on a diet?"

Most of the girls said they were.

"I just want to be skinny so no one will tease me," explained Sara Totonchi.

"Boys expect girls to be perfect and beautiful," said Rozi Bhimani. "And skinny."

I was the questioner that day. As a young *Wall Street Journal* reporter, I had gone to a handful of Chicago-area schools to ask 100 fourth-grade girls about their dieting habits. Researchers at the University of California at San Francisco were about to release a study showing 80% of fourth-grade girls were dieting, and I wanted to determine: Was this a California oddity, or had America's obsession with slimness reached the 60-pound weight class?

My reporting ended up mirroring the study's results. More than half of the 9-year-old girls I surveyed said they were dieting, and 75%—even the skinniest ones—said they weighed too much. I also spoke to fourth-grade boys and learned what the girls were up against. "Fat girls aren't like regular girls," one boy told me. "They aren't attractive."

The front-page story helped spark discussions about America's worship of thinness and its impact on children. It raised the question: Would these girls be burdened by the dieting culture as they grew into women?

Those girls I interviewed are 32 and 33 years old now, and when I got back in touch with some of them last week, they said that they and their peers have never escaped society's obsession with body image. While none of them descended into eating disorders, some told stories of damaging diets and serious self-esteem issues regarding their weight.

[T]oday's fourth-grade girls are barraged by media images of thinness.

They felt—and recent studies make clear—that the weight-focused pressures on young girls today are even stronger. In the now-quaint era of 1986, the girls had told me about drinking Diet Cokes and watching Jane Fonda exercise videos. Ms. Totonchi had read a teen novel about a girl with an eating disorder.

Going to Extremes

But today's fourth-grade girls are barraged by media images of thinness. They can cruise the Internet visiting "Pro-Ana" (pro-anorexia) Web sites and can view thousands of "thinspiration" videos on YouTube celebrating emaciated young women.

"Models look like popsicle sticks," Suzanne Reisman told me in fourth grade. Today, she amends her observation: "Now they look like toothpicks."

In fourth grade, Christy Gouletas told me thin models "are sexy, so boys like them." Today, she is a middle-school teacher in Wheeling, Ill. On lunch duty each day, she notices 10 girls who eat nothing. "We make them take a few bites," she says, "but they fight me on it. They say, 'I'm not hungry,' and I tell them, 'You've been here since 8 a.m. Of course you're hungry!'"

"The influences are worse now," says one researcher, Kerry Cave, a clinical nurse leader at Martin Memorial Medical Center in Stuart, Fla. Earlier this year, in the Journal of Psychosocial Nursing, she chronicled the latest research on "the influences of disordered eating in prepubescent children." Among the findings: A preoccupation with body image is now showing up in children as young as age five, and it can be exacerbated by our culture's increased awareness of obesity, which leaves many non-overweight kids stressed about their bodies. This dieting by children can stunt growth and brain development.

Between 2000 and 2006, the percentage of girls who believe that they must be thin to be popular rose to 60%. . . .

Incidences of bulimia have tripled since the 1980s and anorexia incidences have also risen, according to studies collected by the National Eating Disorders Association. Parental fixations on weight, children's urges toward perfectionism, family conflicts, and a $40 billion-a-year dieting industry can all lead girls to disorders. But studies also show that self-starvation in girls can be triggered by media images, including Internet sites promoting anorexia and bulimia as lifestyle choices. Among the pitch lines used on these sites: "Nothing tastes as good as thin feels." On one recent "Pro-Ana" blog, a woman suggested a 30-hour group fast and received 64 responses such as "I can't wait to do this fast with you. Thirty hours food-free sounds like heaven" and "I'm with you. Down to the bones."

Researchers have seen a marked increase in children's concerns about thinness in just the past few years. Between 2000 and 2006, the percentage of girls who believe that they must be thin to be popular rose to 60% from 48%, according to Harris Interactive surveys of 1,059 girls conducted for the advocacy group Girls Inc.

Compared with the fourth graders of 1986, girls today see body images in ads "that are even further from reality. Retouching is rampant," says Claire Mysko, author of *You're Amazing*, a book encouraging self-esteem in girls. She worries that childhood obesity-prevention efforts can make girls obsessive about weight. While these programs are important vehicles to fight a growing problem, "we have to be really careful how we are implementing nutrition and body imaging," she says.

Then and Now

Those fourth graders of 1986, now all grown up, offer heartfelt reflections on all of these issues.

Ms. Totonchi is public-policy director at the Southern Center for Human Rights in Atlanta. In fourth grade she told me she wanted to be thin so no one would tease her. "What I said that day is still very true," she says. Today, she watches her weight "so I can be successful in a world that puts great emphasis on how a person looks."

She vows to do so through healthy eating. As an adult, she once experimented with a low-carb diet and says she still has high blood pressure as a result. "It did so much damage to me," she says. "It was a lesson to me not to follow fads."

Ms. Reisman, now a writer and blogger in New York, says she was an emotional eater as an adolescent, "turning to food for comfort." She got heavier in college, but she now watches what she eats and weighs a healthy 125 pounds. She is concerned about the heightened pressures on girls today to be thin and sexy. She knows of 9-year-olds asking their mothers to buy them thong underwear. "That's horrifying to me," she says.

Ms. Gouletas, the teacher, says she was "always a fat kid" and is now 40 pounds overweight. Even though she eats healthy food and exercises five days a week, it's hard for her to shed pounds.

As a fourth grader, Krista Koranda recognized that some people can't help being overweight. "We don't make fun of fat girls," she said. Not all her male classmates were as empathetic. One boy in her class responded that if someone can't help being fat, "then you shouldn't make fun of them. But girls in the fourth grade can help it."

Now a public-relations consultant in Boulder, Colo., Ms. Koranda Torvik (her married name) says she appreciates it when ad campaigns today use plus-size models. "That's encouraging," she says, even though such ads are the exception.

In fourth grade in 1986, Ms. Bhimani says, she and her friends admired teen celebrities such as Molly Ringwald, "girls who were skinny but healthy." Now, the actresses on teen TV shows such as the resurrected *90210* are being called "alarmingly thin" in media reports. "They look so unhealthy," says

Ms. Bhimani, an attorney for the Federal Trade Commission in Chicago. "And it's a skinny that's unattainable for most people."

Ms. Bhimani became heavy in college and later took off 40 pounds through exercise and portion control. When she re-read my 1986 *Journal* article, she found some of the boys' comments "appalling." She thought about her 3-year-old son. In six years, he'll be in fourth grade.

"I hope I am able to instill values in my little guy that help him see past weight," she says. "The pressure to stay thin comes from many different sources in society, and I just hope my son isn't one of those sources."

12

Mothers' Obsession with Dieting Harms Sons as Well as Daughters

Renee Martinez

Renee Martinez is a writer, marketing communications consultant, and the mother of four boys. She also writes a blog called Raising Boys World.

In addition to the media's influence on children about "ideal" body images, a mother's attitude about her own body has a huge impact on how sons, as well as daughters, view themselves. Both boys and girls learn by imitating what they see; for example, if they see skipped meals, an interest in calorie-counting, or a negative mindset about weight, that is what they will emulate. As a result, boys can develop eating disorders as readily as girls, and it is important for mothers to be aware of that fact.

While moms with sons may barely give a thought to their boys developing eating disorders or anorexia as compared to moms with daughters, boys and girls feel similar pressures to conform to specific body images. As mothers, we may be focused on health and wellness, but our sons are inundated with images of ideal bodies, weight concerns and sex.

In fact, from a very young age, children are taught that looks matter. With kids watching more television than ever before, their idea of what "normal" is may not be accurate.

When the media depicts overweight males, they tend to associate these images with negative stereotypes such as laziness or inability to attract women, while the "ideal" muscular and lean body is associated with success. And there's the flood of diet advertisements selling anything and everything to lose weight and improve muscles.

What a Child Notices

In addition to media influence, how does a mother's focus on battling the bulge contribute to her son's self image? Dara Chadwick, author of the book *You'd Be So Pretty If...*, says girls formulate their body images relative to how their mothers feel about their own bodies. But what about boys? If a woman raising a boy is a yo-yo dieter or overly concerned about losing weight, what impact does this have on her son? Do boys care? Do they even notice at all?

[B]oys and girls feel similar pressures to conform to specific body images. ...

In *My Mother, My Mirror*, author and therapist Laura Arens Fuerstein focuses a mother's influence over their daughters but makes a point of mentioning that both girls and boys need to feel that their mothers are powerful so that they can feel secure. As a result, what Mom says becomes extremely important; she functions as a mirror reflecting back her child's sense of self.

Psychologists who have studied this process say the influence of the mother is greatest in the years before puberty. We know that children learn by imitating what they see. Since a child is closest to a parent, what a parent does to model behaviors has a big influence on a child. A parent's unresolved body image or negative attitudes towards eating and weight are passed from one generation to the next. While the cycle has a tendency to continue, it can be prevented if the parent with issues works to prevent their child from falling into the same trap.

How do we know when a normal concern (or focus) evolves into an obsession and becomes a problem? There is a fine line between normal and unhealthy eating habits. The determining factor lies in the purpose of why someone eats. Behaviors fall into the category of pathology when a person eats to serve emotions rather than appetite, or is unable to choose his actions freely. Genetics reportedly play a role in eating disorders. The parents are not the reason for causing their child's eating disorder, but their influence can contribute to triggering a child's genetic predisposition toward developing disease.

It's important to remember that if a parent suffers from an eating disorder and chooses to keep it hidden and not seek medical assistance; a child is likely to still learn the parent's actions. A child notices skipped meals, an interest in calorie counting, or the fat-free or light foods in the house. When a child sees that a parent is always on a diet or isn't happy with how she looks, a child experiences anxiety and stress and doesn't learn how to practice open communication.

[M]ales account for up to 25% of anorexia cases.

Setting a Healthy Example

Compound that with the fact that today fewer families share family meals than ever before. Children are more isolated and disconnected from parents and siblings because the prevalence of fast food, separate meal times, eating on the go and eating while watching television. All these behaviors inhibit the socialization that typically occurs when families eat together. As a result, children may wind up experiencing depression, especially when a parent suffers from an eating disorder. If a parent is unable to establish her own self-control, she may have a difficult time setting external controls for her son or daughter. As a result, a child who cannot self-regulate is more likely to develop an eating disorder of his own. When parents try to control their children's food intake by insisting that their children clean their plate, boys are more likely to request larger portions. This interferes with a child's ability to listen to his body and can affect his relationship with food.

Studies published over the last few years suggest that males account for up to 25% of anorexia cases. In fact, it's estimated that as many as 1 million American men have an eating disorder. But because of the perception that it's a female problem, many of them don't seek help. This is not a disease that only affects girls. Eating disorders are about more than just about food. They're also about self image. Sufferers have very low self-esteem.

Boys diagnosed with anorexia may seek zero body fat as compared to their female counterparts who want to be thin. The syndicated TV show *Dr. Phil* tackled the subject of Body-Obsessed Boys in an episode originally broadcast January 8, 2009. On the show, 15-year-old Eric and 22-year-old Troy discussed their struggles battling eating disorders, bringing an issue that receives little media attention to a larger audience.

A mother's influence can certainly have far-reaching effects on her sons even into adulthood. For this reason, it's important for mothers to pay close attention to the examples they set and the comments they make—as well as resolve any personal issues with food and self-image—so that their children will have a better chance at a life free from eating disorders and body image issues.

Organizations to Contact

The editors have compiled the following list of organizations concerned with the issues debated in this book. The descriptions are derived from materials provided by the organizations. All have publications or information available for interested readers. The list was compiled on the date of publication of the present volume; names, addresses, phone and fax numbers, and e-mail and Internet addresses may change. Be aware that many organizations take several weeks or longer to respond to inquiries, so allow as much time as possible.

American Council for Fitness and Nutrition (ACFN)
1350 I St., Suite 300, Washington, DC   20005
e-mail: contact@acfn.org
website: www.acfn.org

The American Council for Fitness and Nutrition (ACFN) is a nonprofit organization working to address the nation's obesity epidemic with practical long-term solutions. The organization collaborates with health professionals, educators, policy makers, and others on comprehensive and sustainable approaches to reducing and preventing obesity. ACFN has produced communication and outreach toolkits and has published the reports "Building Healthy Lifestyles Early in Our Nations Youth: A Call to Action" and "Achieving Energy Balance in the Population: A Solution for the Obesity Epidemic."

American Dietetic Association (ADA)
120 South Riverside Plaza, Suite 2000, Chicago, IL   60606
(800) 877-1600
website: www.eatright.org

With approximately 70,000 members, the ADA is the world's largest organization of food and nutrition professionals. The ADA's commitment to helping people enjoy healthy lives has led the organization to concentrate on the critical health issues of obesity, aging, nutrigenetics, and integrative medicine. The ADA's publications include nutrition fact sheets, position and practice papers, and the monthly *Journal of the American Dietetic Association.*

Healthy Refrigerator

1100 Johnson Ferry Road, Suite 300, Atlanta, GA   30319
e-mail: natlcoordinator@healthyfridge.org
website: www.healthyfridge.org

The Healthy Refrigerator includes nutrition and health recommendations for children and adults along with recipes, articles, and quizzes. A "Just for Kids" section offers facts about heart disease and a "healthy fridge" quiz. Its website provides articles on nutrition and healthy eating.

Mayo Health Clinic

200 First St. SW, Rochester, MN   55905
(507) 284-2511 • fax: (507) 284-0161
website: www.mayoclinic.org

The Mayo Clinic, the first and largest integrated not-for-profit medical practice in the world, is devoted to the diagnosis and treatment of virtually every type of complex illness. Doctors, specialists, and other health care professionals provide comprehensive diagnoses, understandable answers, and effective treatment. The Mayo Clinic has sites in Rochester, Minnesota; Jacksonville, Florida; and Scottsdale-Phoenix, Arizona. The Mayo Clinic publishes the quarterly *Sharing Mayo Clinic,* the *Mayo Clinic Magazine* and the e-mail newsletters *Discovery's Edge* and *Health Policy Center.*

National Association of Anorexia Nervosa and Associated Disorders (ANAD)

PO Box 640, Naperville, IL   60566
(630) 577-1333
e-mail: anadhelp@anad.org
website: www.anad.org

ANAD, a nonprofit organization, strives to educate the general public and professionals by gathering and providing research relating to the causes, prevention, and treatment of eating disorders. In addition to its hotline counseling, ANAD operates an international network of support groups and offers referrals to health care professionals who treat eating disorders. ANAD publishes the national quarterly newsletter *Working Together* and will mail information packets customized to individual needs upon request. It also provides educational speakers, programs and presentations for schools, colleges, public health agencies, and community groups.

National Eating Disorders Association (NEDA)
603 Stewart St., Suite 803, Seattle, WA   98101
(206) 382-3587 • fax: (206) 829-8501
e-mail: info@NationalEatingDisorders.org
website: www.nationaleatingdisorders.org

NEDA is the largest nonprofit organization in the United States dedicated to eliminating eating disorders and body dissatisfaction. NEDA aims to accomplish its goals by promoting positive body image and self-esteem through prevention programs, the distribution of educational materials, research, and a referral line. Among NEDA's publications are toolkits for parents, educators, and coaches, as well as the brochures "What Is an Eating Disorder?" and "How to Help a Friend."

Overeaters Anonymous (OA)
P.O. Box 44020, 6075 Zenith Court NE
Rio Rancho, NM   87144-6424
(505) 891-2664
e-mail: info@overeatersanonymous.org
website: www.oa.org

OA is a nonprofit international organization that provides volunteer support groups worldwide. Modeled after the 12-step Alcoholics Anonymous program, the OA recovery program addresses physical, emotional and spiritual recovery aspects of compulsive overeating. Members are encouraged to seek professional help for individual diet and nutrition plans and for any emotional or physical problems. The organization publishes the *Courier* newsletter for the professional community and the quarterly newsletter *A Step Ahead* for OA members.

Society for Adolescent Health and Medicine (SAHM)

111 Deer Lake Rd., Suite 100, Deerfield, IL 60015
(847) 753-5226 • fax: (847) 480-9282
e-mail: info@adolescenthealth.org
website: www.adolescenthealth.org

SAHM is a multidisciplinary international organization of professionals committed to improving the physical and psychosocial health and well-being of all adolescents. It helps plan and coordinate national and international professional education programs on adolescent health. SAHM's publications include the monthly *Journal of Adolescent Health* and the quarterly *SAHM Newsletter*.

Something Fishy

P.O. Box 837, Holbrook, NY 11741
(866) 690-7239
website: www.something-fishy.org

Something Fishy is dedicated to raising awareness of eating disorders and emphasizing that eating disorders are neither about food nor weight. Something Fishy is determined to remind every eating disorder sufferer that he or she is not alone, and that complete recovery is possible. The organization publishes *In Their Words*, which are short stories and articles written by those suffering or in recovery, and the newsletter *Positive Voices*.

United States Department of Agriculture (USDA)

1400 Independence Ave. SW, Washington, DC 20250
(202) 720-2791
website: www.usda.gov

The USDA promotes US agricultural products and provides information pertaining to nutrition, obesity prevention, meal planning, and food labels. The USDA website also includes multiple food pyramids designed to outline the nutrition needs of various age groups. Among the USDA's publications are the reports "Dietary Guidelines for Americans," "Nutritive Value of Foods," and the briefing "Diet Quality and Food Consumption."

Vegetarian Resource Group (VRG)

P.O. Box 1463, Baltimore, MD   21203
(410) 366-8343
e-mail: vrg@vrg.org
website: www.vrg.org

VRG is a nonprofit organization dedicated to educating the public on vegetarianism and the interrelated issues of health, nutrition, ecology, ethics, and world hunger. VRG runs the Vegetarian Resource Group blog and publishes a newsletter, the *Vegetarian Journal,* and various guides and handouts, including "Heart Healthy Eating Tips" and "Vegan Diets in a Nutshell."

Bibliography

Books

Linda Bacon

Health at Every Size: The Surprising Truth About Your Weight. Dallas: Ben Bella Books, 2010.

Dawn Jackson Blatner

The Flexitarian Diet: The Mostly Vegetarian Way to Lose Weight, Be Healthier, Prevent Disease, and Add Years to Your Life. Columbus, OH: McGraw-Hill, 2010.

Sheryl Canter

Normal Eating for Normal Weight: The Path to Freedom from Weight Obsession and Food Cravings. New York: Permutations Software, Inc., 2009.

Dara Chadwick

You'd Be So Pretty If . . . : Teaching Our Daughters to Love Their Bodies—Even When We Don't Love Our Own. Cambridge, MA: DaCapo Press, 2009.

Brian M. Delaney and Lisa Walford

The Longevity Diet: The Only Proven Way to Slow the Aging Process and Maintain Peak Vitality. Cambridge, MA: DaCapo Press, 2010.

Roberta Larson Duyff

American Dietetic Association Complete Food and Nutrition Guide. Hoboken, NJ: John Wiley & Sons, 2006.

Laura Arens Fuerstein   *My Mother, My Mirror: Recognizing and Making the Most of Inherited Self-Images.* Oakland, CA: New Harbinger Publications, 2009.

Elson M. Haas   *Staying Healthy with Nutrition: The Complete Guide to Diet and Nutritional Medicine.* Berkeley, CA: Celestial Arts, 2006.

Kate Harding and Marianne Kirby   *Lessons from the Fat-O-Sphere.* New York: Penguin Group, 2009.

Jane R. Hirschmann and Carol H. Munter   *Overcoming Overeating: How to Break the Diet/Binge Cycle and Live a Healthier, More Satisfying Life.* Philadelphia: First DaCapo Press, 2008.

Mayo Foundation for Medical Education and Research   *The Mayo Clinic Diet: Eat Well, Enjoy Life, Lose Weight.* Beaverton, OR: Good Books Publishing, 2010.

David A. Kessler   *The End of Overeating: Controlling the Insatiable American Appetite.* New York: Rodale, 2009.

Paul McGlothin and Meredith Averill   *The CR Way: Using the Secrets of Calorie Restriction for a Longer, Healthier Life.* New York: Harper Collins, 2008.

Stuart A. Seale, Teresa Sherard, and Diana Fleming   *The Full Plate Diet: Slim Down, Look Great, Be Healthy!* Austin, TX: Bard Press, 2010.

Alicia Silverstone — *The Kind Diet: A Simple Guide to Feeling Great, Losing Weight, and Saving the Planet.* New York: Rodale Books, 2009.

Dianne Neumark-Sztainer — *"I'm, Like, SO Fat!": Helping Your Teen Make Healthy Choices About Eating and Exercise in a Weight-Obsessed World.* New York: Guilford Press, 2005.

Periodicals

Victoria Anisman-Reiner — "Disadvantages of Going Veg: A Guide to Those Considering the Health Impact of Vegetarianism," Suite101.com, February 12, 2007.

Judith Beck — "Stress and Emotional Eating: Using Cognitive Behavior Therapy to Break the Habit," PsychologyToday.com, November 24, 2010.

Jane E. Brody — "Paying a Price for Loving Red Meat," *The New York Times*, April 27, 2009.

Laura A. Cassiday — "The Curious Case of Caloric Restriction," *Chemical & Engineering News*, August 3, 2009.

Maria Cheng — "Global Obesity Rates Have Doubled Since 1980," Associated Press, February 4, 2011.

Matthew Dalton — "Fighting Obesity May Take a Village," *The Wall Street Journal*, November 10, 2009.

Matt Frazier	"How a Vegetarian Diet Can Make You a Better Endurance Athlete," LivingHarvest.com, August 8, 2010.
Kathy Freston	"Why Vegan Is the New Atkins," HuffingtonPost.com, July 23, 2008.
Audrey Grayson	"Best Diet: Low-Fat, Low-Carb or Mediterranean? Research Belies Long-Held Belief that Low-Fat Diets Are Best," ABCNews.com, July 16, 2008.
Nanci Hellmich	"'Cleansing' Diets Lure Celebs, but Not Health Experts," *USA Today*, March 24, 2009.
Aimee Christine Hughes	"Eat Less, Live Longer," *Seattle Woman*, January 2010.
Claudia Kalb	"Culture of Corpulence: American Innovations in Food, Transportation, and Technology Are Threatening to Supersize Us All," *Newsweek*, March 14, 2010.
Barbara Kantrowitz	"Too Good to Be True: Why Some Over-the-Counter Diet Pills Aren't Just a Sham, They're Downright Dangerous," *Newsweek*, April 1, 2009.
Natasha Mann	"How Our Vegan Diet Made Us Ill," *The Independent*, June 17, 2008.
Camille Noe Pagan	"A Body Cleanse that Isn't Crazy," *Women's Health*, April 2010.

Tara Parker-Pope   "In Obesity Epidemic, What's One Cookie?" *The New York Times*, March 1, 2010.

Christine Schrum   "Raw Food Diets: Pros and Cons," *The Iowa Source*, August 6, 2009.

Katherine Seligman   "Iron Will: Can a Diet of a Quarter Fewer Calories than a Body Needs Lead Boomers to that Ever Elusive Fountain of Youth?" *San Francisco Chronicle*, September 2, 2007.

Richard Sine   "Detox Diets: Purging the Myths," WebMD.com, reviewed May 12, 2009.

Rebecca Traister   "Diet Your Way to a Long, Miserable Life!" Salon.com, November 22, 2006.

Irina Webster   "Eating Healthy: Does Extremely Healthy Eating Lead to Eating Disorders?" Associated Content, June 16, 2008.

Jessica Yadegaran   "Obesity Epidemic Hits the Diaper Set," *Contra Costa Times*, January 30, 2011.

Index